# THE BRITISH ARCHITECTURE & INTERIOR

ブリティッシュ・アーキテクチュア&インテリア

coordinated by
**Fumio Shimizu**+**Deyan Sudjic**

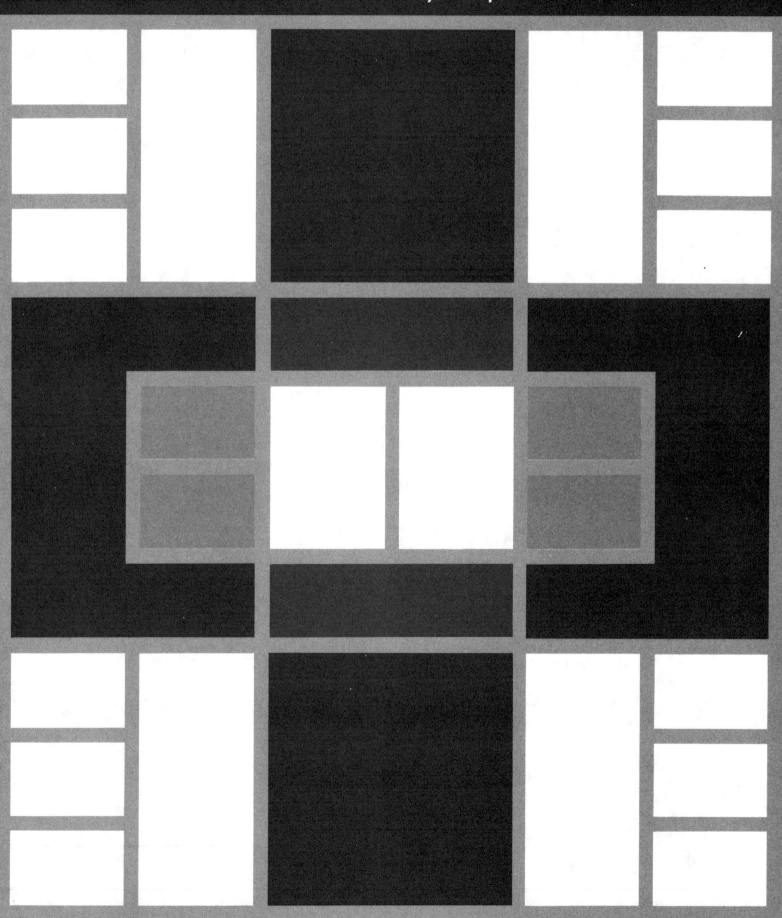

# THE BRITISH ARCHITECTURE & INTERIOR

# CONTENTS
目次

# Architects and the Pioneers of the A.A. School

Peter Cook (Architect and Professor of A.A. School)

◎ The currently fashionable term "Deconstruction" could never have been applied to any architecture without the phenomenon of London. Nearly all its prime sources stem from a period when the Architectural Association (the famous "A.A.") School held within its bosom Rem Koolhaas, Bernard Tschumi, Elia Zenghelis, almost all of the members of "Archigram" as well as the younger students-who-became-teachers: Peter Wilson, Nigel Coates, Zaha Hadid, Peter Salter, Christine Hawley and Christopher Macdonald.

◎ This is fact.

◎ In a way, this conglomeration of people (who are now mostly building in Germany or Japan and sadly not much in England) existed along-with the English scene and in some ways despite it.

◎ Nowadays the strongest aspect of the London scenery is in the speed with which a streetwise public bypasses the leadership of the great Fashion Houses......and just improvises clothes of wit (and occasional extreme vulgarity). It bypasses the handed-down and over processed atmosphere of the American music scene and just "bashes out" something new (of sometimes extreme banality). In the graphic scene the spot, jump, tweak approach means that things are never boring (though occasionally of extreme obscurity). Perhaps the most inventive designer around is Ron Arad (taught by Bernard Tschumi and myself at the A.A.) who treads into architecture, hi-fi, sculpture, light-art and then into a vision more of the City of the Future than anyone else if you start to put together his robot arms and shimmering swathes and flexing seats.

Typically, he is an import. None of the English people mentioned come from London and the rest are forigners who like to stay despite the extraordinary manner of the English in not noticing when you do something interesting. It is of course, the corollary of not noticing when the clothes-music-graphics are vulgar-banal-obscure as much as pretending not to notice the positive qualities. "Get on with it, but don't expect me to like it" is the cry.

◎ Of course, in recent times. London has acquired a posse of quite sophisticated architects and designers such as Chipperfield, Conder, Powell-Tuck, Davies and the like who produce with great skill and retain London as a "design" city though, for me, their work lacks the inheritance of a "funky" quality that one finds in the real inventors like Arad, Hadid, Gough or Peter Salter.

◎ Perhaps the London effect is best characterised by Peter Wilson, An emigre from Melbourne, he graduated from the A.A. alongside Nigel Coates in a period strongly involved in the magic of symbolic objects, poetry, romantic allusions and gentle objects. He rapidly moved out from this into the creation of beautiful projects such as the Fountain House and the Venice bridge. With his German architect wife, Julia Bolles he entered competitions — notably that for the Tokyo Theatre which were always arresting and the obverse side of a powerful influence that he held as a teacher. The Wilson studio at the A.A. in the mid 1980's was sheer poetry. Winning the competition for the City Library of Munster in West Germany was the great breakthrough......a building of substance and power as well as retaining the delicate formal poetry of earlier work. It is now being built, though threatening the consistent presence of Wilson in England. Indeed, Will Alsop, Peter Wilson and Myself are very frequently seen on the Lufthansa airline.

◎Meanwhile the three Giants continue to flourish: Stirling and Wilford, Rogers and Foster have built up such a strong trajectory that London is automatically a World Centre of architecture without any support from the rest. More particularly interesting is the existence of a "technical quadrilateral" that exists between the offices of Rogers and Foster and those of Nicholas Grimshaw and Michael Hopkins. Almost an "Academy" in its own right, it surreptitiously encourages (or at least creates) all sorts of cloning, industrial espionage and good, straightforward back-and-forth movement of staff. So it is possible to identify a London architectural type the "Tech" architect who will have as much inherited expertise with microchips, gaskits, trusses and perforated metal as did those products of IIT in the Chicago of the 1950's and 1960's who inherited from Mies van der Rohe. Another story, sometime, needs to be written about the underbelly of this British (High) Tech Academy — which is really to be found in the engineers that are there. Peter Rice, Tony Hunt, Frank Newby, Ted Happold, Mark Whitby......to name only the best known. Somehow, the same audacity that we see in clothes, music and graphics was present in the extreme inventiveness of English and Scottish engineers in the 19th century and has been inherited by these men. Extreme, experimental and naughty things are done that can only be a challenge to their architect partners.

◎Nonetheless, I have the suspicion that the pressure of politics, banking and survival are puitting a great pressure on English architects. Added to this is a strong feeling around that you have to conform to get along. So we see more and more neat looking architects with the right computer terminal and the right cut of suit replacing the hairy, jagged individual......rather the pattern of New York or Tokyo, perhaps.

◎Where are the embryo Nigel Coates followers of NATO. There is so far no new challenger to Archigram, NATO, or even the earlier vulgarity (but power) of CZWG.

◎England might be the ideal place however, for the final blood to be spilled at the death of Postmodern architecture. Just as the hallowed Prince Charles becomes more and more powerful and populist with his attack upon new architecture (he hates everyone in this book) and just as he advocates more and more horrible alternatives, there are signs that the middle-ground of Postmodern is getting pushed to the High Streets. Silly already it will be revealed as base fashion — maybe for the wrong reasons (of sheer fashion replacement) but also because it cannot offer operational solutions for a world that will demand more machine flexibility, image transference and witty space.

◎By the way, you will notice that I have not really mentioned England......only London. There isn't much going on up there that would interest outside observers, except perhaps for Glasgow......another naughty twon, culturally and in the architects' department of the

Hampshire County Council!

◎ If you come to London however, you will notice one thing, that I have only otherwise noticed in Los Angeles, and that is that the Lion will sit down with the Lamb. There is no-one in this book who would walk out of the bar if the other walked in! People carry on a discreet English-style non-debate with each other......even Zaha Hadid (who is not a meek person) will hold fire in London on occasion. To explode is a sign of weakness. To try to react to the studied ignoring is a sign of weakness too. Nobody will stop you designing anything there......but to get it built......now that implies recognition.

◎ Meanwhile there are some extraordinary things done by London architects — and located outside London, mostly. Ian Ritchie's Eagle Rock house in Kent. Alsop and Lyall's swimming pool in Sherringham. Michael Hopkins' Schlumberger factory near Cambridge. Fisher Park's creation for pop music and, still the best, the extraordinary juxtaposition of a magical black blob in an undistinguished provincial town......the Foster offices in Ipswich......the Martians did arrive and live on.

Tokyo, May 1989                                    Peter Cook

# 建築家とロンドンのA.A.スクールの先駆者たち

ピーター・クック（建築家・A.A.スクール教授）

◎目下ファッショナブルなものとして擁護される「デコンストラクション」は、ロンドンでのこの現象がなければ、絶対にどの建築にも適用されることがなかったであろう。そのあらゆる源は、A.A.（アーキテクチュラル・アソシエーション）スクールにおいて、のちに教師になった若手の学生たち、ピーター・ウィルソン、ナイジェル・コーツ、ピーター・ソルター、クリスティーナ・ホーレイ、クリストファー・マクドナルドらばかりでなく、レム・クールハース、バーナード・チュミ、エリア・ゼンゲリスなど「アーキグラム」のほとんど全メンバーを育んでいた時代に根ざしている。

◎このメンバーは、現在ほとんどがドイツか日本で仕事をしており、悲しいことにイギリスにはあまり残っていない。しかし、この集団は、イギリスのシーンとともに、存在したのである。

◎現在ロンドンの情景の最も強烈な面が現れるのは、町の事情に通じた大衆が大きなファッション・ハウスのリーダーシップを無視し……気まぐれで、雑で、即興的に衣服をつくりだすスピードにおいてである。この大衆はアメリカの音楽シーンのお下がり的な、過剰処理を無視し、ただ何か新しい、時にははなはだ陳腐なものを叩きだすだけである。グラフィック・シーンにおいては、テンポの早い、ちょっとひねったアプローチは、物事が決して退屈させないことを意味する。ことによると最も創意に富むデザイナーは、A.A.でバーナード・チュミと私に教わったロン・アラッドかもしれない。彼は、ハイ・ファイ、彫刻、ライトアートへと進み、そして、もし彼のロボットの腕と光る包帯と曲る座席をいっしょに組

み立てるなら、他のだれよりも未来の都市のヴィジョンにはいりこんでいる。典型的に、彼は外からやって来た人間である。ここにあげたイギリス人はひとりとしてロンドン出身ではなく、残りは外国人でイギリス人に風変わりなやり方にもかかわらず、そこに留まり、何かに夢中になっているときはそんなことは忘れている。ファッション、音楽、グラフィックは、積極的な性質に気づかないふりをするだけでなく、野卑で陳腐なあいまいさをもつとき、それはもちろん気づかないことの結果である。「それとうまくつきあっていける。しかし、わたしがそれを好きになることを期待しないでほしい」というのがその叫びである。

◎もちろん、最近、ロンドンにはチッパーフィールド、コンダー、バウエル・タック、デイヴィスやその他、優れた技術で制作し、ロンドンを「デザイン」都市として保っている人たちのような高い見識をもった建築家やデザイナーの集団ができた。だがしかし、私には彼等の作品がアラッド、ハディド、ゴフやピーター・ソルターのような真に発明の才のある人たちに見られる「素朴な」性質を受け継いでいないと思われる。

◎おそらくロンドン効果はピーター・ウィルソンに最もよくその特長がでている。メルボルンから移り住んだ彼はナイジェル・コーツとともに、象徴的な事物の魔術、詩、ロマンティックな引喩および優しい事物に強くかかわりあった時期に、A.A.を卒業した。彼は速やかにこうしたものから抜けだして、ファウンテン・ハウスやベニス・ブリッジのような美しいプロジェクトの想像にはいった。建築家であるドイツ人の妻、

ジュリア・ボレスとともに彼はコンペティションに参加した——特に東京劇場のためのものがある——それからは常に注目をひき、彼が教師としても強い影響力をもつことになる。1980年代のA.A.におけるウィルソン・スタジオは純粋な詩であった。西ドイツミュンスターの私立図書館のコンペティションに優勝したことは、大きなブレーク・スルー……初期の作品の繊細で形の整った詩を残しながら、実態と力の建物となったのであった。図書館は目下、建築中であり、そのためウィルソンはいつもイギリスにいるというわけにはいかない。事実、ウィル・アルソップ、ピーター・ウィルソンと私はしばしばルフトハンザ航空機の客となるのである。

◎その間、スターリングとウィルフォード、ロジャースとフォスターは他から何の助けがなくても、ロンドンを自動的に建築世界の中心にのしあげるような強烈な軌道をつくりあげた。とりわけ興味深いのは、ロジャースとフォスターのオフィスおよびニコラス・グリムショーとマイケル・ホプキンスのオフィスの間に存在する「技術の四辺形」の存在である。自分たちだけの力でできた「アカデミー」といっていいほどで、あらゆる種類を、そっくりまねるとか、産業スパイをやるとか、スタッフが悪巧みなしに行き来する動きを内々に奨励する。それゆえロンドンの建築のひとつのタイプを「テク」の建築家と判定することが可能である。彼はミース・ファン・デル・ローエから、1950年代と1960年代におけるシカゴのIITの製品と同じように、マイクロチップやガスキャットやトラスなどについての多くの専門的知識を受け継いだ。いつかはこのブリティッシュ・ハイテク・アカデミーの弱点について改めて書く必要があろう——それは、そこのエンジニアたちの中に実際にみつけることができる。ピーター・ライス、トミー・ハント、フランク・ニュービイ、テッド・ハッポルド、マーク・ウィットビーなどが有名なところである。なぜか、ファッションや音楽やグラフィックにみられるあの同じ大胆さが、19世紀のイングランドやスコットランドのエンジニアの著しい発明の才にあって、それがこれらの人々に受け継がれているのである。極端で、実験的な冒険がなされて、それがパートナーである建築家に対する挑戦となりえるのである。それにもかかわらず、政治や銀行の問題がイギリスの建築家たちに大きな圧力をかけていると私は密かに思っている。これに加えて、うまくやっていくには順応しなければならないという強い意識がある。それゆえ、コンピューター・ターミナルをもち、きちんとしたスーツを着込み、アカ抜けた建築家が、ニューヨークや東京によくいるみすぼらしい格好の個人にとって代わろうとしている。

◎NATOにおいてこれから育つべきナイジェル・コーツの後継者たちはどこにいるのだろうか？　今までのところアーキグラム、NATOやCZWGの初期の野卑さ（しかしパワーはある）にさえ、新しく挑戦するものがいないのである。

◎しかしイギリスはポスト・モダン建築の死に際して、最後の血を流す場所としては理想的かもしれない。チャールズ皇太子がますます力強く、人民党のように新しい建築に攻撃を加え（彼はこの本に出てくる人々を全部嫌っている）、それにとって代わる恐るべき怪物を擁護する声が高まるにつれて、ポスト・モダンの中道は高みへとおしやられていく兆候があ

る。馬鹿げたことであるが、すでにそれはファッションとして表れるだろう——たぶん単なるファッションの入れ替えというだけでなく、**機械的な融通性とイメージの転換**、そして**機知にとんだスペースを要求する**世界に対して、戦略上での解答をだせないという理由からである。

◎ところで、私がイギリスのことについて、ロンドンをあげただけで、実のある話をしていないことにお気づきだろうか。文化的に向こう見ずな町、グラスゴーとハンプシャー州会の建築家部門を除いて、外部の観察者の興味を引くものはそんなに行われていない。

◎しかし、ロンドンに来れば、気づくことがひとつあるだろう。私がそれに気づいたのはロサンゼルスだけであった。それはライオンが子羊とともにすわっているということである。本書に出てくる人々は、入ってきた人を見て、バーから出てくるような者はひとりとしてない。人々はお互いに論議しない慎重なイギリス式の態度を身につけており(けっしておとなしいわけではない)、ザハ・ハディドでさえ、ロンドンでは時として事実を隠して話さないでいる。爆発するのは弱さのしるしである。学識者たちを無視することで対応しようとするのも弱さのしるしではないだろうか。そこにはあなたが何かをデザインすることを止めるものはおらず……つくらせておく……ということが承認を意味するのである。

◎その間のロンドンの建築家によってなされた——大部分はロンドン以外の地ではあるが——並外れた仕事がいくつかある。ケントにおけるイアン・リチーのイーグル・ロック・ハウス、シュリンガムにおけるアルソップとリアルの水泳プール、ケンブリッジ近郊におけるマイケル・ホプキンズのシュランバーガー工場、フィッシャー・パークのポップ・ミュージックのための作品、そして最高傑作は、地方の町にはめったに見られない、火星人が本当にやってきて、ずっと住んでいる魔術的で、黒の小球体のイブスウイッチのフォスター・オフィスである。

# Complication Caused by Tradition and Individuality

Deyan Sudjic (Critic)

◎Nowherer is Britain's deep seated ambivalence to change more sharply exposed than in its attitude toward architecture. Since the industrial revolution, it is a country that has always been ready to embrace innovation, when it has been presented as commercially expedientwhether it has been the steam engine or the video casette recorder or the microwave oven. But Britain maintains the polite fiction that really nothing has changed. That it is culturally unaffected by the change brought about by these innovations.

◎The motorcar, the facsimile machine, the jet, to name but a few, have inevitably involved massive social dislocation. They have changed forever the way life is lived in Britain's towns and cities. But the British have insisted on ignoring all the changes that technology and demographics bring in their train. Instead they have focussed on architecture. Of all the engines driving the pace of change in modern society, architecture is clearly among the least significant. But it is the one at which the British have drawn the line. To a remarkable degree, the national concensus focusses only on buildings when it becomes aware of its rapidly changing way of life. It is not modern buildings that have created the dispersed, anonymous modern city. Life has beome more brutish, but it has also become more convenient, But the British, are unprepared to do without their motorcars, or mass tourism, out of town hypermarkets. Instead they fondly believe that they can banish all the unpalatable realities of the present, simply by insisting that new buildings conform to some arbitrary idea of tradition.

◎In fact that is exactly what the Prince of Wales is attempting to do with his no doubt entirely sincere crusade for a return to the familiar virtues of the classical past. But in fact, what he is objecting to is not twentieth century architecture, but the 20th century itself.

◎It is a byproduct of the Prince's intervention into the architectual debate in Britain that cynical commercialism has had a much easier ride than the work of those architects who attempt to design buildings that they believe in. This phenomenon reached its peak at the end of the 1980s, when, with more than one in every three buildings in the city of London being rebuilt, and the whole traditional structure of the city breaking down, the only subject of serious debate was James Stirling's plan for the Mappin and Webb triangle next to the Bank of England. While the city authorities eagerly embraced millions of square metres of crude mediocre commercial development without a word of protest, for sites just a few paces away, a modest, dignified scheme of limited size, designed by James Stirling, widely regarded as not just the leading British architect of his time, but among the most distinguished architects of the 1980s internationaly too, became the subject of a fierce three year long legal battle.

◎In the eyes of Prince Charles, and a large section of the British puiblic, Stirling's scheme became the focus for all their angst on the direction the modern world was taking. For hour after hour costly lawyers argued about the colour of Stirling's window frames, and the form of his elevations as if it was the root of all the modern evils.

◎ Something of the same spirit can be seen in the reaction to two almost contemporary London buildings, the Lloyd's insurance market, designed by Richard Rogers, and the Richmond Hill development designed five years later in 1984. The Rogers building is popularly seen as the epitome of high tech, uncompromisingly modern, the symbol of all that is new. While Terry's development with its neo Palladian brick and stucco elevations by contrast is presented as embodying a return to the "traditional" values. In fact, nothing could be more "traditional" than Rogers' building. Behind the technological expressionism of its stainless steel facades, is an ancient City institution building itself a tailor-made landmark headquarters on a site in the centre of London that it has occupied for hundreds of years.

◎ Quinlan Terry's building on the other hand could hardly be more thoroughly modern. Its facades may recreate the 18th century, but the essential idea behind the building, an out of town office block with air conditioning, built speculatively by an office developer with the idea of letting it to tenants as yet unknown is the most modern of ideas. And it is its fundamentaly anti urban qualities which are the real threat to the traditional idea of the city, not the superficial style of Lloyds.

◎ And yet British architecture retains its bloody minded independence. Its architects from Piers Gough to David Chipperfield, from Peter Cook to James Stirling retain a capacity to surprise and shock, to amuse and entertain. Its a country in which the architect at his best, retains an important measure of control on how buildings are actually made. The Lloyds building is in many ways craft work. Its quality depends on the painstaking care with which the architects have played the leading role in designing at a detailed level, not just the general elevations and the plans but the door handles and the specially made triple glazed cladding panels. Its a country which boasts both the worst and the best in architectural educastion. And despite the prejudice against architecture by its ruling elite, there are signs that a new, younger generation of architects now in its mid 30s is beginning to make its presence felt. Unlike its predecessors in the 1960, the new generation of architects in Britain is building commercial work, not social housing: evidence of the changing nature of British society.

◎ It has its enfants terribles, and its heroic form givers, as well as its high tech wizards, and its cheerful charlatans. It has its home grown post odernists, who look to America for inspiration, but it is the sophisticated updating of modernism as practised by Norman Foster and Richard Rogers, coupled with James Stirling's independent minded stance that have really attracted attention internationally for British architecture. Encouragingly, there are signes of a new generation emerging from under their wing.

# 伝統と自立の葛藤

ダヤン・スジック〔評論家〕

◎イギリスの建築に対する態度ほど、変化に対するアンビヴァレンスが激しく現れるところはない。産業革命以来、この国は蒸気機関であろうと、ビデオであろうと、電子レンジであろうと、便利で経済的なものは、いつも新しいものを進んで受け入れてきた。しかし、イギリスが古来よりもつ体質は何も変わってはいないという、上品な伝説をひきずっているのである。こうした技術革新がもたらした変化によって全く文化的な影響を受けていないのである。

◎自動車、ファクシミリ、ジェット機など登場によって、社会に大きな動揺をもたらした。これらはイギリスの町や都市での今までの暮しぶりを全く変えてしまった。しかしイギリス人は執拗に、テクノロジーと人口統計の数字がもちこんだあらゆる変化を無視しつづけ、彼らは建築に攻撃の的を絞ったのである。現代社会の変化の速度をはやめる機動力のうちで、建築は最も意義の少ないものと認識された。しかし、それはイギリス人が一線を画したもののひとつである。顕著にみられることだが、ナショナル・コンセンサスは暮し方の急激な変化を意識するとき、建物だけに集中する。バラバラで個性のない現代都市をつくりだしたのは現代建築ではない。生活は一段と便利になるが、また一段と野卑になる。しかしイギリス人は自動車や観光旅行や郊外のスーパーマーケットなしで暮す覚悟がない。その代わりに、彼らは新しい建物に伝統というあいまいな基準を強制することで、現代のこの不快な状況を払いのけることができると信じているのである。

◎事実、チャールズ皇太子が古典的な過去の懐かしい美徳を復古させるために、疑いもなく真剣に復興運動を展開しよう と試みているのがそれである。しかし、このことは20世紀建築に反対しているのではなく、20世紀そのものを否定しているのである。

◎チャールズ皇太子が建築についての討論に介入したことの副産物は皮肉なコマーシャリズムのほうが、自らの信念に従って建物をデザインしようとする建築家よりもはるかに御しやすいということがわかったことだけだった。この現象が頂点に達したのは、1980年代の終わり、ロンドン市内の建物の3分の1以上が改築され、市の伝統的構造全体が崩れて、ただひとつ真剣に討論されたのが、イングランド銀行の隣のマピン&ウエブ・トライアングルのためのジェームズ・スターリングによるプランがだされたときに、最高潮に達した。市当局が一言の抗議もなしに、何百万平方メートルもの粗雑で、月並みな営利的開発に熱心に取り組む一方で、ほんのわずかな敷地のために、当代指折りのイギリス建築家であり、国際的にも名高い建築家のひとりであるジェームズ・スターリングが設計した、控え目で気品のある企画が3年の長きにわたり激しい法廷争議の的となっているのだ。

◎チャールズ皇太子をはじめ、イギリスの一般大衆の目にはスターリングの企画は現代社会の明日への不安を体現するものとして映ったのである。費用のかかる弁護士たちが、スターリングのウインドー・フレームの色、正面の形などとりあげて、まるでそれが現代の諸悪の根源かのように、何時間もかけて、攻撃した。

◎このような精神が、ほぼ同時期に、リチャード・ロジャースの設計によるロイズ・保険マーケットと、5年おくれて設

計されたリッチモンド・ヒル開発に対する反応に現れている。ロジャースの建物は一般にハイテクの典型、現代的で、新しいものの象徴とされている。他方ネオ・パラディアンれんがとスッタコの正面をもつテリーの開発は、対象的に「伝統的な」価値への復帰を象徴するものとして認識されている。実際にはロジャースの建物以上に「伝統的」なものはないのである。ステンレス・スチールのファサードの技術的表現主義の背後にかくれているのは、古いロンドンの機関の建物そのもの、それが何百年もの間ロンドン中央部の敷地に建ち、それに合わせた歴史的建造物の本部となっているのである。

◎他方クインラン・テリーの建物はこれ以上ないほどにモダンである。ファサードは18世紀を再現しているが、背後にある基本的なアイディア、テナント貸しにするという考え方、オフィス・デベロッパーが投機的目的に建て、空調設備をそなえた町はずれのオフィス・ブロックは、最も現代的な考え方である。この都市の伝統的なアイディアに真の脅威となるのは、ロイドの表面的なスタイルではなく、テリーの本質的に反都会的な傾向である。それでもなお、イギリスの建築は、その猛烈な独自性をもち続ける。ピアーズ・ゴフからデイヴィッド・チッパーフィールド、ピーター・クックからジェームズ・スターリングまでの建築家は人々に衝撃をあたえ、楽しませてくれる能力をもち続けている。イギリスは頂点に立つ建築家が建物の現実的な建て方をコントロールする重要な尺度をもっている国である。ロイズ・ビルディングはいろいろな点で工芸品である。その品質は隅々にいたるまで、建築家主導の配慮がなされている。それは総合的な立面図や平面図にかぎらず、ドアのハンドルや特製の外装パネルまでにもおよぶのである。イギリスは建築教育において、ピンからキリまでを自慢にする国である。一般のエリート意識による建築への偏見にもかかわらず、今や30歳代の半ばに達した建築家たちの、新しい世代が台頭し始めている。1960年代における彼らの先駆者たちとは違って、新しい世代のイギリスの建築家たちは社会的な住宅建築でなく、営利的な作品を多くつくりだしている。これはイギリス社会そのものの性質が変わっていくことの証拠であろう。

◎イギリスはハイテクの魔法使いと陽気な山師ばかりではなく、恐るべき子供たち、冒険的なつくり手たちをかかえているのである。自国で育ったポスト・モダニズムをもっているが、彼らはアメリカにインスピレーションを探し求めようとする。イギリスの建築に対して、実際に国際的な注目をあつめたのは、ノーマン・フォスターとリチャード・ロジャースが実践したようなモダニズムのアカ抜けした改訂版であり、それと対になるジェームズ・スターリングの独立精神旺盛な姿勢である。楽しみなのは、新しい世代が彼らの庇護のもとから離れ巣立ちつつあるということである。

Explanatory Notes:
凡例

P : ............................ Project/プロジェクト
T : ............................ Title/タイトル
D : ............................ Designer/デザイナー
C : ............................ Client/クライアント
L : ............................ Location/所在地
A : ............................ Area/エリア
M : ............................ Material/マテリアル

Editorial Director　Kakuzo Akahira
エディトリアル・ディレクター　赤平覚三

Book Design　Toru Kaiho
ブック・デザイン　海保 透

Typesetter　Tatsuya Yoshida (Miyama Total System Co.,Ltd.)
タイプ・セッター　吉田達也（株式会社三山綜合システム）

Translation　AKKORD Co.,Ltd.
翻訳　アコールト株式会社

Cooperation　Aleph
協力　アレフ

Cover Works
カバー使用図版

a: FOSTER ASSOCIATES
b: POWELL-TUCK, CONNOR＋OREFELT LTD.
c: WILLIAM ALSOP＋JOHN LYALL ARCHITECTS
d: ZAHA HADID
e: ARMSTRONG ASSOCIATES
f: STANTON WILLIAMS
g: FISHER PARK LTD.
h: PAWSON SILVESTRIN

## THE BRITISH ARCHITECTURE & INTERIOR
Copyright © 1989 Graphic-sha Publishing Co.,Ltd.
1-9-12, kudankita, Chiyoda-ku, Tokyo 102, Japan
ISBN4-7661-0545-1

Printed in Japan
First printing, 1989

# WORKS

# ANDREW HOLMES
## アンドルー・ホームズ

P : Design studio
T : Lapot
D : Andrew Holmes
C : Lapot
L : London
A : 140m$^2$
M : Steel, Glass, Birch Faced Plywood

◎ボッタの椅子は低コストの合板を使うことにより、円筒状の会議室をこのスペースの中央の主眼として配置した意味を明確にし、付属家具としての外観を保っている。

Botta's chairs contrast the low cost plywood used to define the cylindrical meeting room which acts as centrepiece to this space and helps define the form of the accompanying fittings.

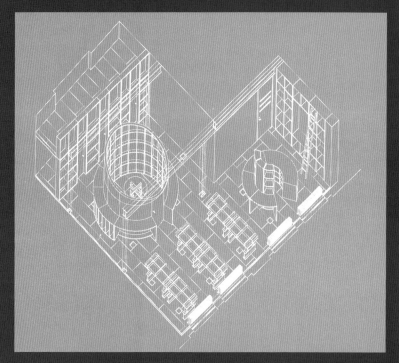

P : Illustration
T : Great Dane
D : Andrew Holmes
P : Illustration
I : Meat market(Video drawing)
D : Andrew Holmes
P : Illustration
I : Steinbecker Bros.
D : Andrew Holmes

◎ 建築ドラフトマンとしてのホームズの器用さは、彼がグラフィック・アート、イラストレーションの世界で自他ともに認められる経歴に根ざしている。

Holmes' dexterity as an architectural draftsman originates from his Graphic, illustrative background for which he is recognized in his own right.

P : Conceptual work
T : Making other arrangements
D : Andrew Holmes
L : London

◎ この設備はベッドフォード広場に取りつけられ、独立したスペースとしてその広場の本来の性質を表現している。

This installation was built in Bedford Square and relates the true nature of that square as an independent space.

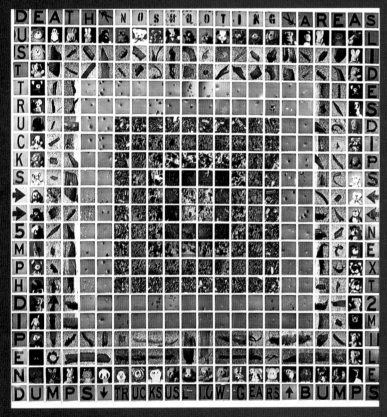

P : Design Studio
T : 7A Langley street
D : Andrew Holmes
C : Brewer Jones and Partners
L : London
A : 370m$^2$
M : MDF Steel Rod, Carpet, Tiles

◎ ミニ摩天楼は収納ユニットとガラスのテーブル
・トップを支える台の二役をする。デザイナーは
それぞれ1街区を占有し、クライアントが大規模
な開発を行うように、自分の必要や情熱のおもむ
くままに開発することができる。
◎ 実際に動くクレーンが調整可能なテーブル・ラ
ンプの役をしている。

The mini skyscrapers act as storage units
and supports for the glass table tops.
Each designer is able to occupy a city
block and develop it according to his or
her needs of enthusiasms just as a client
might with a full scale development.
The functioning cranes serve as
adjustable table lamps.

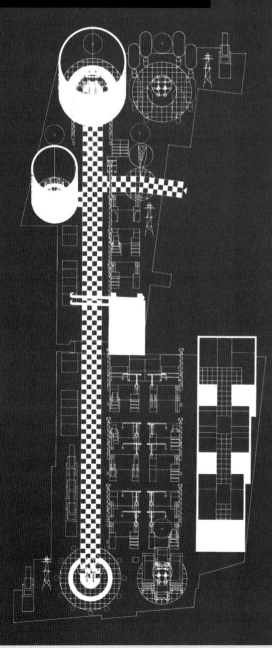

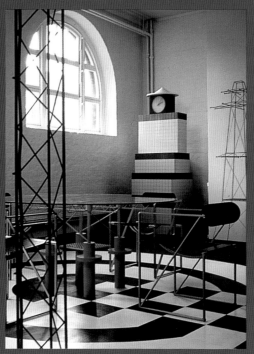

# ARCHITEKTURBURO BOLLES WILSON
## アーキテクトゥルビュロー・ボレス・ウィルソン

P : Bridge/Building
T : Bridge Building No.4 Il Ponte Dell'
    Academia
D : Architekturburo Bolles Wilson
C : La Biennale Di Venezia
L : Venice
A : 120m²
photo by Richard Davis

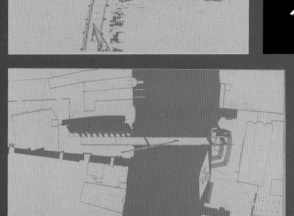

◎ブリッジ・ビルディングという名がこのデザインの基本的コンセプトを説明している。つまりブリッジであり、ビルディングでもある。実際にはブリッジとギャラリーである。基本的に異なる要素を意図的に並置し、相互作用と、各々の機能的に相容れない対立が、全体の豊饒化を促進している。このブリッジは歴史的に隣のアカデミアの名を引き継いでおり、今またその機能を引き継いでこのように公共の場にまでのびている。こうした仮設は刺激的である。それは現代の状況を認め（ブリッジ、観光客、芸術の宝、ベニス・ビエンナーレ）、新しい、そして現代的なビルディング・タイプを生みだしている。

◎新しいブリッジは、構造的にその場所の不均斉を反復する。構造は片持ち梁で、3本のプレストレスト・コンクリートのビームが指のように壁から飛びだしている。この細さは最高で、このために余分な構造上の支え、フライング・トラスを必要とした。この要素は構造と装飾の両方をかねている。グランド・カナルという歴史的なスペースへの20世紀の無言の侵入であり、それでも、祝祭日にはつつましやかに、旗やのぼりを掛ける竿の役目をはたしている。

The title Bridgebuilding describes the fundamental concept of this design, it is both bridge and building, bridge and gallery infact. Such a juxtaposition of essentially dissimilar types is intentional, promoting an enrichment through interaction and an intensity of occupation that each would not have as functionally separate entities. The bridge having historically taken on the name of the adjacent Accademia now also takes on its function thus extending it into the public realm. Such a hypothesis is intentionally provocative. It allows the contemporary situation, (bridge, tourist, art treasure, Venice Biennalle) to generate a new and contemporary building type. Structurally the new bridge reiterates the asymmetry of the site. It is a cantilever, three prestressed concrete beams springing fingerlike from the wall building. The thinness of this line is paramount, so mach so that it is slimmed down to the extent that it needs extra structural support, the flying truss. This element is both structure and figuration. An unapologetic twentieth century intrusion into the historic space of the Grand Canal, and yet on festive days it modestly preforms the role of coathanger for flags and banners.

P : Mews House
T : Blackburn House
D : The Wilson Partnership with Chassay Wright
C : Mr & Mrs D W Blackburn
L : London
A : 190m²
M : Plastered Brick, Wooden Paneling, Steel
    Furniture
photo by Richard Davis

◎ この家の妥協のない形と細部は、表通りから見えないという理由で、建築に対する保守的、反動的な土地柄のロンドンで可能となった。ファサードはすべて斜めであり、既存の構造の細部をはぎとり、無秩序な窓を塗り込め、壁を高くし、真っ白な箱、手品の箱、おもちゃ箱をつくりだしている。

◎ 箱の中のおもちゃは現代の家具である。大部分はこの家のために特に製作を依頼したもので、ワン・オフのロン・アラッド作のテーブル、芸術家ブルース・マクリー作のサイドボード、ジャスパース・モリソンのソファ、フローレンス・ヴァン・デル・ブルックのデスクがある。敷地もまた、フラナガン、ウォールホールその他の作品でデザインされている。14mの盲壁の、だが天窓のある上階は、主要なギャラリー・スペースとして、下のロビーはチェア・ホールとして機能している。他方でベッドルームと書斎は特有な設計物、ベッドとデスクを収納している。白く、抽象的な箱とその中味の対照は絶対的ではない。細部までの正確さと高品質を求めるクライアントの条件から、小規模な建物の改造が許可された。ガラスの飾り戸棚や、スチールのバルコニーのようなものが、他の家具と並び、他方突き出た窓や、木のパネルをはめた書斎のボトル型プランは、箱であることを強調している。

The uncompromising form and details of this house are only possible in the reactionary and architecturally regressive climate of London because it is unseen from the street, the facade is always oblique. The existing structure has been stripped of details, its chaotic windows blinded, its walls raised to create a clear white box, a box of tricks, a toy box. The principle toys in the box are contemporary furniture. Most pieces have been commissioned specifically for this house, a table by Ron Arad (of One Off), a side board by the artist Bruce McLean, a sofa by Jasper Morrison, a desk by Flores van der Brucke. Sites have also been designed for pieces by Flanagan, Warhol and others.
The upper floor with its 14m blank but skylit wall functions as the principle gallery space, the lower lobby as chair hall, while bedroom and study frame their single specific designed object, bed and desk. The distinction between the white, abstract box and its contents is not absolute. Requirements by the client for precision and high quality details gave licence for the development of small scale architectural objects; some like vitrine and steel balcony take their place with the other furniture, while larger elements like the projecting window or the bottle plan of the wood panelled study are expressive qualifications of the box.

facade to mews

upper floor

window seat

entrance hall

stereo & portait

balcony

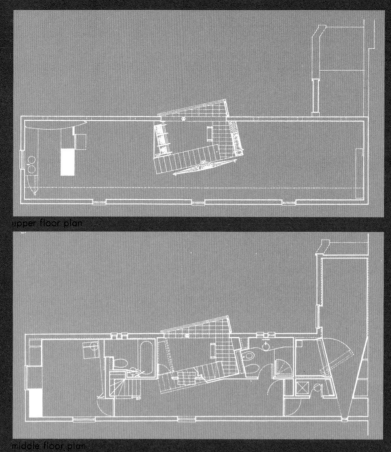

upper floor plan

middle floor plan

balistair detail

P : Libary
T : Munster Library
D : Architekturburo Bolles Wilson
C : Stadt Munster
L : Munster
A : 10,000m²
M : Concrete Plasered Walls, Copper Walls

entrance

◎新しいミュンスターの市立図書館は、現在をそこに描きながら、幾層ものレベルで、その歴史的かつ文脈的な状況に応える、新しい層を重ねている。その構成は伝統的な図書館のモデル（知識の館、書籍の館）に、活動的なゾーン、情報ゾーン（メディア・シュトラーセ）を伴い、必然的に拡張した。新しい図書館のためのコンセプト全体は、この基本的な区分から発すると理解してよい。

◎図書館の内部は旅、つまりひとつの事件を象徴している。外部は複雑で、歴史に敬意をはらいつつ、現代を強く主張している。図書館の各ゾーンの配置は連続した構成となり、公共のスペースはカフェ・テラスまでのび、メディア・シュトラーセは情報（図書館についてだけでなく、市自体についても）を提供する。目録（情報ゾーンのバルコニーにある）から、橋（ランベルティ教会の眺め）が書架へと通じる。このゾーンの中央で、書物と建物は一体となって壁となり、それを囲んでいくつかの閲覧サロンが集まっている。ここでは、機械についての本や、東京についての本、電子の映像についての本が読まれるのである。

The new City Library in Munster is a new layer, descriptive of the present and yet responding on a number of levels to its historic and contextural situation. The program involved the expansion of a traditional library model (house of knowledge/house of books) to include a more active zone, a zone of information (the Media Strasse). The whole concept for the new library can be understood as originating from this fundamental division. The interior of such a library is a journey, a sequence of events. The exterior is complex, historicaly respectfull but also insistantly modern. On entering the disposition of zones like the library program is sequential. Public spaces extend out to the cafe terrace, the Mediastrasse presents information (not only about the library but also about the city itself). Then from catalogues (on the balcony of the information zone) the bridge (view of Lamberti Church) leads to the bookstacks. At the centre of this zone books and building combine as backbone wall (full with shelves) and surrounding it are grouped the various reading salons. Here books will be read, books about machines, about Tokyo, about electronic shadows and about the Grossstadt itself.

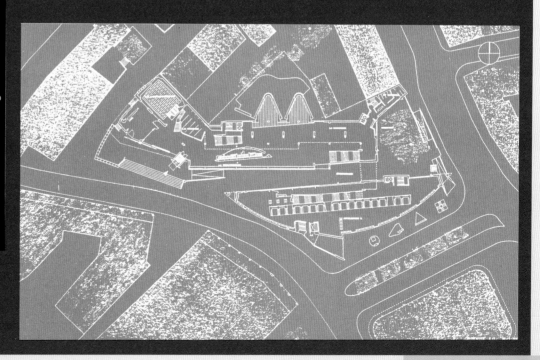

courtyard elevation

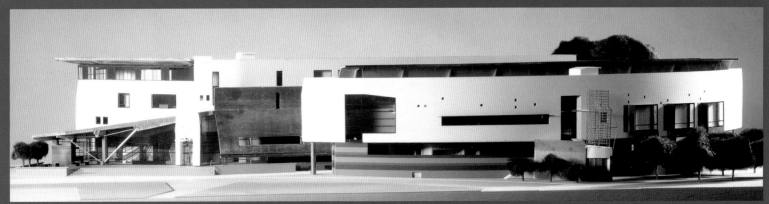

south elevation

# ARMSTRONG ASSOCIATES
## アームストロング・アソシエーツ

P : Office/Showroom
T : Elementer Industrial Design Limited,
    Headquarters Building
D : Armstrong Associates
C : Elementer Industrial Design Limited
L : Berkshire
A : 576m²
M : Painted Plaster, Etched Glass Douglas Fir,
    Danish Oak, Spruce Pine, MDF Board,
    Portland Stone, Marble, Stainless Steel
photo by Richard Bryant

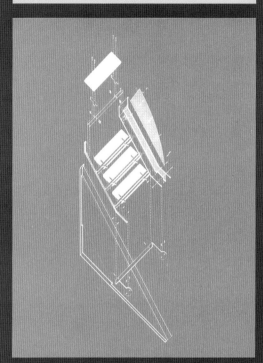

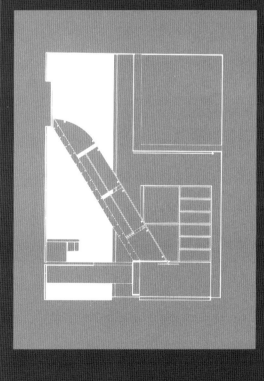

◎クライアントの条件は、新しい2階建の工業用計量ユニットを使用して、エレメンター社の重役オフィスなどのスペースから、倉庫や保管スペースまでを設計してほしいというものであった。デザインはエレメンタリー社の製品に合わせ、実際にはショールームとして使用できるものとした。

◎レイアウトはコンセプトにおいても手法においても単純で、様々な天然素材を用いている。

◎機能を割り振るにあたり、応接間とショールームを1階の入口の隣に配置した。会議室との境は2枚の大きな引戸で仕切られ、レセプションなどのときは開け放たれる。倉庫への入口は別に建物の裏側にある。

◎むきだしのオーク材の踏板がついた、ステンレス・スチールとガラスの階段を上ると2階がオフィスである。階段はステンレス・スチールのフラットをD字型のボルトで止め合わせたもので組み立てられている。強化ガラスのパネルが切り梁風につき出たステンレス・スチールの手摺を支えている。両者とも階段の基部に沿ってカーブさせてある。

The client's requirement was for the architect to create from the shell of a new 2-storey light industrial unit, a space for each section of the Elementer company — boardroom, director's offices etc. through to warehouse and storage space. The design was to be sympathetic to the Elementer products — in effect a working showroom. The layout is very simple in conception and execution, incorporating a rich variety of natural materials.

The functions are arranged so that the reception and showroom are located adjacent to the entrance on the ground level, separated from the boardroom by two large sliding doors, which are opened for social events, receptions etc. A separate entrance to the warehouse is located at the rear of the building.

A stainless steel and glass staircase with open oak treads leads up to the offices on the second floor. The staircase is assembled from stainless steel flats bolted together using a version of the d-line 'pig-head' bolts. The toughened glass panels support a cantilevered stainless steel handrail, both are curved to meet the base of the stair.

staircase detail

office

staircase detail

entrance

main staircase

handrail detail

reception area

P : Hairdressing Salon
T : Neville Daniel
D : Armstrong Associates
C : Neville Tucker and Daniel Hercheson
L : London
A : 450m²
M : Painted Plaster, Etched Glass Terazzo,
    Stained Hardwood, Stainless Steel

◎ 裁断室はお客のひとりひとりに対しうちとけた
スペースを提供するために、4室ずつまとまって
配列されていて、見た目の清潔さと、手入れのし
やすさ、耐久性で選ばれた白いテラゾのフローリ
ングにしている。そのフローリングが背後のエリ
アの後ろまでのびている。1階レベルで、持ち上
がったプラットホームとして表現されている。裁
断室はライトグレーのラッカーで仕上げ、上部は
床表面のテラゾを繰り返し、他方、ふんだんに使
用された鏡が、逆光で照らされた食刻ガラスの板
を組込み、単純な、互いに連結する平面群となっ
ている。
◎ 1階の裁断エリアから、2階の高さのスペース
が立ち上がり、2つの中二階エリアをつなぐスチ
ールとガラスの通路が横切っている。このいちだ
んと高いレベルからは、段のある壁面装飾が周り
を囲んで3つの側面から中央のスペースが見下ろ
され、まるで劇場のような景観を呈する。

The cutting stations, mostly arranged in
clusters of four to provide intimate and
individual areas for each client, sit on
white terazzo flooring, selected for its
clean appearance, ease of maintenance
and durability. The same flooring extends
up to and behind the backwash areas
and is expressed at first floor level as a
raised platform. The cutting stations are
conceived as simple interlocking planes,
with a light grey lacquered finish, the
tops echoing the terrazzo of the floor
surfaces, while the generous mirrors
incorporate vertical strips of backlit
etched glass.
From the first floor cutting area the
double height space rises up traversed by
a steel and glass walkway linking the
two mezzanine areas. From this upper
level the central space takes on an almost
theatrical aspect, overlooked on three
sides with a stepped mural completing
the enclosure.

staircase landing detail

furniture detail

cutting station

P : Office
T : Financial Institution
D : Armstrog Associates
C : Banco de Portugal Competition Entry
L : Portugal
M : Steel, Aluminium, Glass.

◎ アームストロング・アソシエーツの最初の大規模プロジェクトは、フィージビリティ・スタディとヨーロッパの主要な金融機関のための新しい本部建物の設計とを包含している。提案では、この機関のおもな機能を営業施設と社会的、文化的施設との2つに分けている。前者は、ほぼ100万平方フィートの質の高いオフィス設備である。広々とした庭園風の中庭と内部のガラス板をはめたアトリウムの周りに並び、アトリウムの下は広い地下室である。後者は公立博物館、図書館および庭園に面するスポーツセンターを含んでいる。

Armstrong Associates first large scale project comprises a feasibility study and design for the new Headquarters building for a major financial institution in Europe. The proposal separates the 2 major functions of the organization into the operational facilities and the social and cultural facilities. The former comprising approximately 1 million square feet of high quality office accommodation arranged around an open, landscape courtyard and internal, glazed atrium with extensive basements below, and the latter including a public museum, library and sports centre facing onto a landscaped garden.

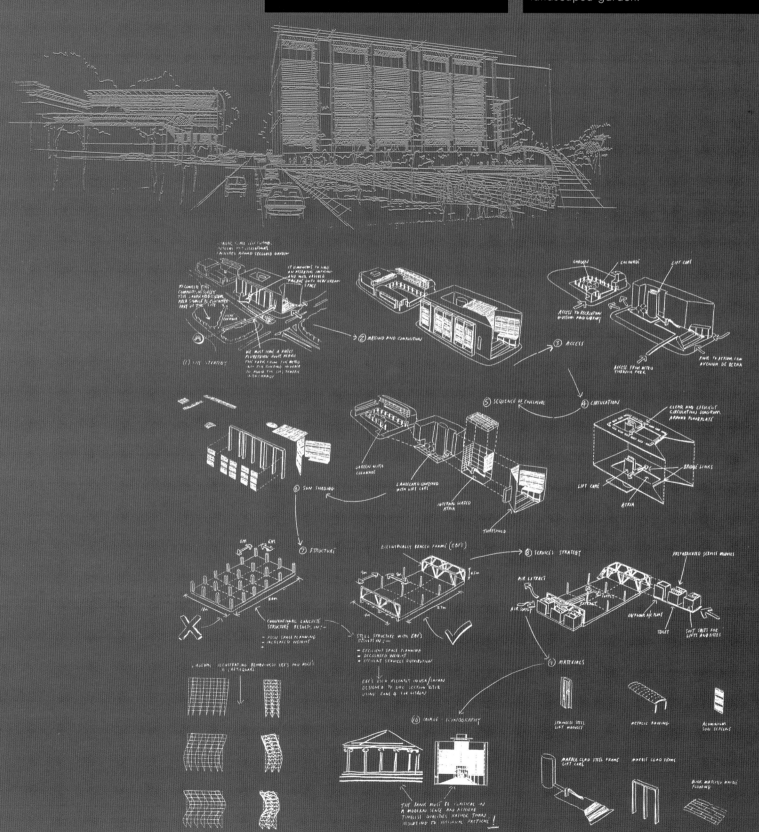

# BEEVOR+MULL ASSOCIATES
ビーヴァ+マル・アソシエーツ

P : Restaurant, Bar, Cafe
T : The Coleville Rose
D : Beevor+Mull Associates
C : Adam Kidron/Courage Ltd.
L : London
A : 350m²
M : Plywood, Upholstery

◎今やボヘミアンに侵略されて、人種のるつぼと化したロンドンのポートベロにあるバー、コルヴィル・ローズはかつて、あまり評判のよくない、みすぼらしいパブであった。現在は、2階を私的なダイニング・クラブ、街路面はバーとカフェになった。
◎限られた予算は有効に使われた。スペースや素材の使い方は大胆かつ簡素となった。上階では既存の部屋のレイアウトはほとんど変えられなかった。バーは合板と布を張った家具にすぎず、シャンデリアは既製品の部品でできている。
◎階下は陳腐さをもてあそび、英国のパブのもつ男っぽさとくだらなさを表現し、さらにそれを現代的な手法で解釈し直そうとしている。それゆえバーは周囲を圧倒し、どっしりとしたドアは特大かつ頑丈である。彩色した壁は明るいカリブ風である。合板の壁には風刺的な「階級的フラストレーション」をのぞき見る窓があり、友人が上階のエリート意識へこそこそ逃げていくのを見ることができる。工業部品を組み合わせライトボックスをつくり、家具は明るいイタリアの路上カフェ用のものをまねている。

Found in Portobello, a racially mixed area now well infiltrated by London's bohemia, the Coleville Rose caters to all. Converted from a seedy, disreputable public house, it now provides a private dining club on its second floor. and a bar and cafe at street level.
A limited budget was positively exploited; use of space and materials is necessarily bold and simple. Upstairs the existing layout of rooms was little changed. The bar is just a piece of ply and upholstered furniture, the chandelier only made from mass produced components.
Downstairs plays with the banal; it purposefully edges toward the masculinity and kitsch of all British pubs but tries to reinterpret the tendency with crisp modern means. So the bar is tall and dominant; the massive entrance doors are also over scaled and sturdy. Coloured walls are bright and carribean, the ply walls frame peep windows for satirical 'class frustration': spot your friends sneaking away to the elitism of upstairs. Industrial components are adapted to make the light boxes; the furniture is plagiarized from sunny Italian sidewalk cafes.

quilted bar detail

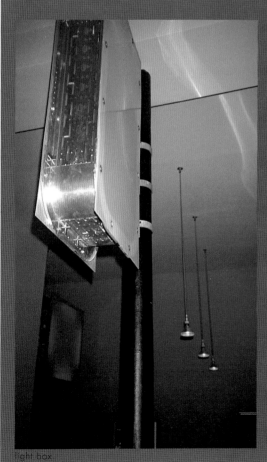

light box

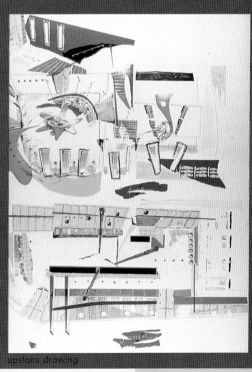

upstairs drawing

P : Audio And Visual Recording Facility
T : Orinoco
D : Beevor+Mull Associates
C : Tom Astor
L : London
A : 750m²
M : Concrete Blocks, Plywood Panels,
    Aluminium, Acoustic Panels

トム・アスターはビーヴァ+マルにまずオリノコのコンセプトを相談した。建築家たちは彼とともに研究し、オーディオ・ビジュアル結合レコーディング施設の概要をつくり上げた。彼らは恰好の場所、改造を必要とする旧ミッション・ホールと外の建物をバーモンゼーでみつけた。

それは若々しく、強靭で、あかぬけたものにすることを狙って設計された。最も熱狂的なスターの激しい動きにさえも傷まない構造になっている。裸のコンクリートブロック、合板張りの壁、スレートの表面、上張りをした防音パネル、可動のアルミニウム・スクリーン、補強用ロッドのレール、工業用照明備品、湾曲した銅製ラジエーター、砂漠色の構成、失われたロンドンを偲ばせる様々な引き揚げられた記念物、すべてが緻密で一風変わった設計を強調している。

オリノコはロンドンで一番人気のあるレコーディングとビデオ、TVスタジオであり、ブライアン・フェリー、ヤズ、ジョージ・マイケル、ゲイエ・バイカース・オン・アシッド、シューガー・クラブなどが使っている。

Tom Astor consulted Beevor and Mull at first conception of Orinoco. With him, the architects researched and formulated the brief for a combined audio and visual recording facility. They found the site, an ex mission hall plus out buildings in Bermondsey, ripe for conversion.
It was designed to be young, tough and smart; the fabric is not hurt by the worst behaviour of the wildest stars. Find there bare concrete blocks, ply panelled walls, slate surfaces, upholstered acoustic panels, mobile aluminium screens, rails of reinforcing rod, industial light fittings, curling copper radiators, a desert colour schele and various salvaged mementoes of lost London, all punctuating light and unusual planning.
Orinoco is London most popular recording and video/TV studio, used by (og) Bryan Ferry, Yazz, George Michael, Gaye Bykers on Acid, The Sugar Cubes.

sound studio

chandelier

skylight

staircase & door

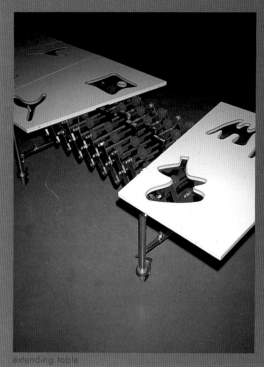

extending table

reception & bar

P : Photographic Studio
T : LWM/The Presentation Works
D : Beevor+Mull Associates
C : LWM Photographers
L : London
A : 350m²

◎これは改造したビクトリア朝倉庫のインテリアの一新である。クライアントは商業写真家たちで、彼ら自身で処理・製造を行っている。
◎ビーヴァ＋マル・デザインは既存の土地建物の論理的な利用を提案した。彼らは強力な「自由に動く」建築エレメントを使って活動を組織し、分類した。計画では、アングルは歪められ、軸は強調され、色彩は辛辣、すべてが処理プラントとオフィス・テクノロジーの中立性を克服し、若く順調な会社に秩序とアイデンティティーを与えることを目ざしている。

This is an interior refurbishment of a converted Victorian warehouse. The clients are commercial photographers with their own very sophisticated processing and production operation. Beevor and Mull's design proposed a more logical use of their existing premises. They have used strong 'free floating' architectural elements to organize and categorise activities. In plan, angles are distorted, axes exaggerated and colours are acidic, all to cut through the neutrality of processing plant and office technology, to give order and identity to a young and successful company.

screen & rails

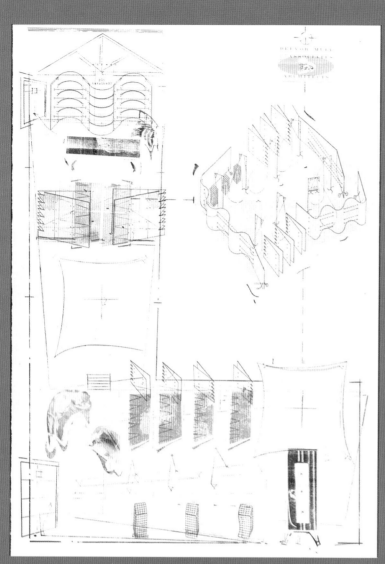

fire lobby

storage wall

# BEN KELLY DESIGN
ベン・ケリー・デザイン

P : Bar/Brasserie
T : Dry
D : Ben Kelly Design with S.Douglas,
    E.Massucco, P.Mance and D.Byrne
C : FAC 201 Ltd.
L : Manchester
A : 700m²
M : Mild/Stainless Steel, Slate, Glass, Telegraph
    Poles, Japanese Oak, Douglas Fir, Utile,
    Glazed Bricks, Stained Plaster

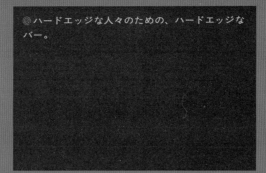

◎ハードエッジな人々のための、ハードエッジなバー。

A hard edged bar for hard edged people.

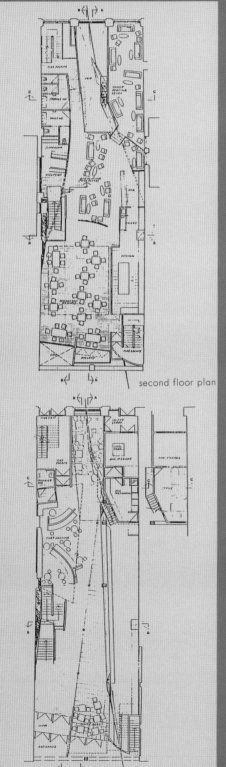

second floor plan

first floor plan

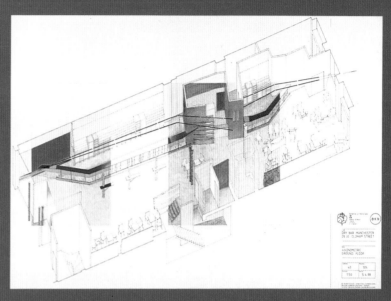

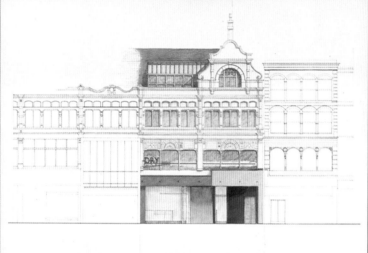

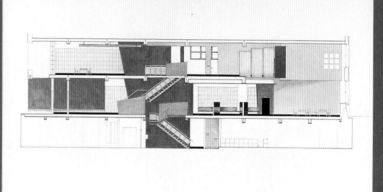

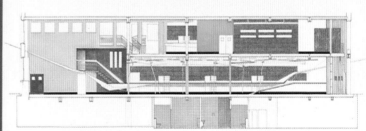

P : Hairdressing Salon
T : Smile
D : Ben Kelly Design, Colaboration: Sandra
    Douglas
C : Keith Wainwright, Lesley Russell
L : London
A : 169m$^2$
M : Bird's Eye Maple Veneer, Granite, Slate,
    Acid Etched Glass, Steel and Concrete
    Stairs

◎ヘア・ドレッシング・サロンをヘア・ドレッシ
ング・サロンらしく見せないひとつの試み。スタ
イリング・ポジションはそれぞれ異なるジオメト
リーをもつが、素材という共通語で統一されてい
る。

An attempt to make a hairdressing salon
look unlike a hairdressing salon. Each
styling position has a different geometry,
but is united through a common language
of materials.

shop front

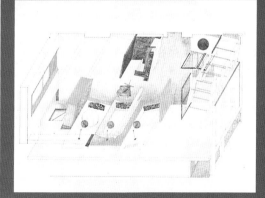

rear staircase

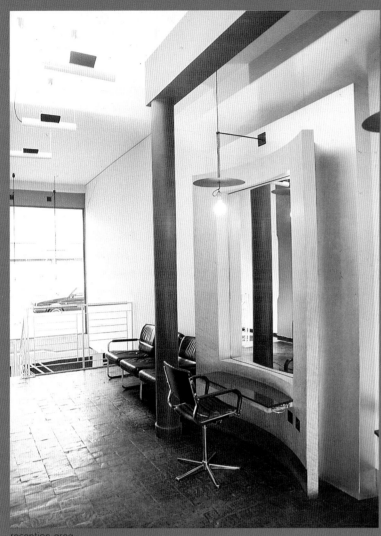

reception area

staircase & basement

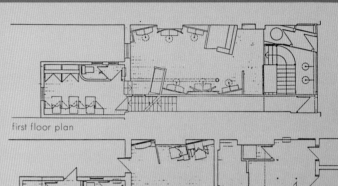

first floor plan

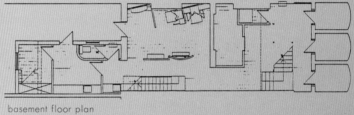

basement floor plan

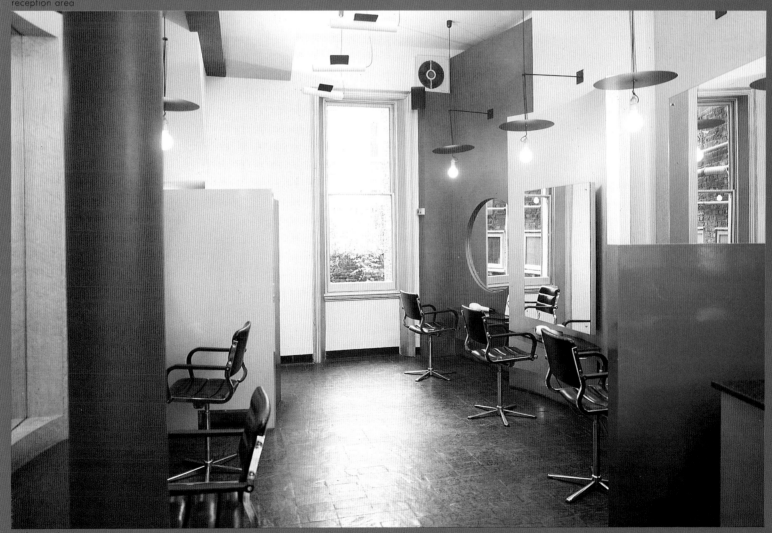

cutting station

P : Shop
T : Quincy
D : Ben Kelly Design with S.Douglas, P.Mance,
    J.Smith
C : Pickwick Clothing Ltd.
L : London
A : 70m²
M : Sandstone Wall, Pear Veneer Cupboards
    and Celling, White Colourcore Wall,
    Stainless Steel Shelving and Hanging Rails,
    Marbo Lapistone Floor, Wenge Shelving,
    Pine Sash Window

◎伝統的な紳士用品商と現代版のコンビネーショ
ン、off set on ceiling fault line？ジオメトリーの
衝突と文脈のないエレメント。

A combination of traditional gentlemans'
outfitters and an updated version, off set
on a ceiling fault line, with a collision of
geometry and elements out of context.

hanging rails

window display

shelves

# BENSON+FORSYTH
## ベンソン＋フォーサイス

P : Oratory
T : Boarbank Oratory
D : Benson+Forsyth
C : Boarbank Nursing Home/Sisters of Mercy
L : Cumbria
M : Curved Etched Glass, White Painted Steel, Ash

photo by Richard Bryant

◎この小礼拝堂のためわれわれが第一に目ざしたのは、その中に入れば、信仰や宗教への傾倒、態度にかかわりなく、自己のほかにある何者かと心を通わせられる聖域をつくりだす、そしてそのコミュニティから発散する愛と生活の質を体現し、物質的な環境をつくることであった。
◎礼拝堂が別個の部屋だと識別できること、また全体の形から細部に到るまであらゆる面がナーシング・ホーム中の同種のエレメントのいずれとも似ていないことが肝要であった。

Out primary ambition for the Oratoty was to create a sanctuary within which, irrespective of beliefs, religious commitment or attitude, one could relate to something outside oneself, and to make a physical environment which embodied the love and quality of life which emanates from the Community. It was essential that the Oratory could be identified as a room apart, and that/ every aspect from the overall form to the smallest component/was unlike any similar element throughout the Nursing Home.

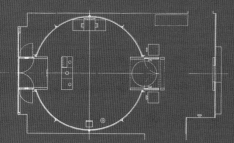

P : Science Market/Commercial Development
T : College Street Development
D : Benson＋Forsyth
L : Scotland
A : 34,000m$^2$

◎この建物の一般的な目的は、商工業と特別な連繋をつくりあげる可能性をもっている大学の学部と資源を設備して、市内に将来の富と誇りを生みだし、アイディアと産業の苗床となるべき環境を用意することにある

◎またこの建物は大学と市の企業との間の、目に見えない絆がグラスゴー市民に、明確に目でとらえられ、理解されるようにする手段とならなければならなかった。

◎それゆえ、チャレンジは建築による環境をつくりだすことにあるのだが、設備として、象徴的な意味あいをもたせようとする機関にはぴったりした、先行の手本が市内にないのである。

The general purpose of the building is to accommodate the departments and resources of the University which have the potential to develop specific links with industry and commerce: to provide an environment which will serve as the seed bed for the ideas and industries which will generate the future wealth and pride within the City

The building should also become the means through which the invisible relationship between the University and the enterprise of the City can be tangibly witnessed and understood by the citizens of Glasgow.

The challenge therefore is to develop an architectural environment which accommodates and symbolically represents an institution for which there is no precise model of precedent within the City.

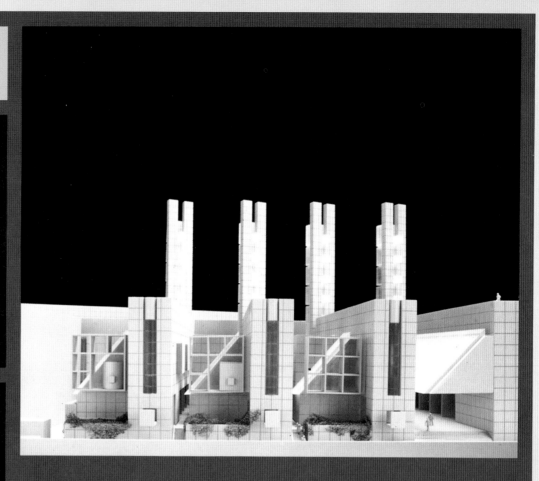

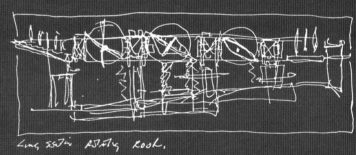

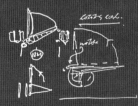

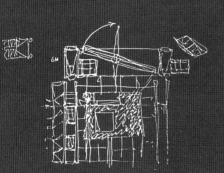

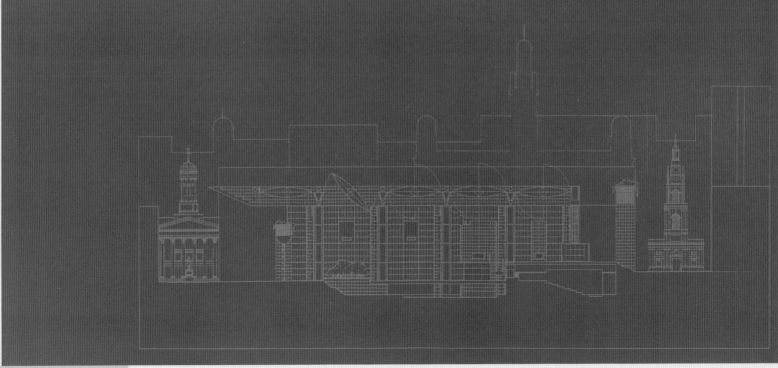

# BRANSON COATES ARCHITECTURE
## ブランソン・コーツ・アーキテクチュア

P : Shop
T : Silver, Jewellery Shop
D : Branson Coates Architecture
C : Bernard and Nick Silver
L : London
A : 62m²
M : Joinery···Walunt, Brass, Glass/Floor···
Parqnay Wood/Facade···Steel with Brass
Details
illustration by Courtesy of Victoria and Albert
Museum

P : Restaurant
T : Arca di Noe
D : Branson Coates Architecture
C : Jasmac Co.,Ltd.
L : Sapporo
A : 500m$^2$
M : Gunite, Sandblasted Wood
photo by Satoshi Asakawa

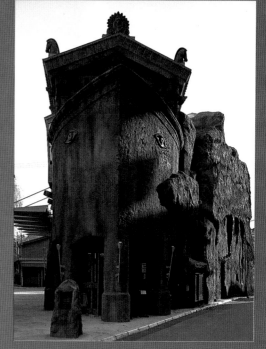

# CAMPBELL ZOGOLOVITCH WILKINSON | GOUGH
## キャンベル・ゾゴロヴィッチ・ウィルキンソン＋ゴフ

P : Private House
T : House For Janel Street Porter
D : C.Z.W.G.
C : Janet Street Porter
L : London
A : 100m²
M : Brick＋Brockwork, Precast Concrete, Self Coloured Plaster
photo by Tim Street-Porter

◎外部壁面は、クリーム色から暗褐色までの４色のレンガでグラデーションをつけ、陽の当たる面と影の面という効果をだしている。窓は規則正しく配置され、スチール枠のマリオンに使用されている模様を組合せ、菱形の大きな幾何学模様で飾られている。バルコニーとテラスの手摺となるマッチングのスクリーンが全体の形を仕上げている。窓の横は向側にある公園に敬意を表して、丸太を型どったカスト・コンクリートである。角の斜面は、２階と３階のバルコニーを支えている。下のバルコニーはスペイン風で、適度な高さをもつ手摺で囲まれ、小さな方形をつくりだす。上のものは大きな三角形となり、居間から突き出ている。この階にはもう１つキッチンから出るバルコニーがあり、歩道の上に張りだした円錐状のシートの形をしている。急勾配の屋根は濃い青色の、バンタイルで築かれ、最上階のスタジオ・スペースをつくっている。家の西側の壁面は丸くカーブして、隣の建物の裏側の窓から採光できるようになっている。内部の階段は、この階段に沿って長くゆるやかな曲線を描き最上階に達し、２階に踊場がある。これが内部プランの形を決定する大きな要因となっており、階によってかなり変化がでてくる。

Externally the elevations are brick in four colours from dark brown to cream in gradual changes up the building, which gives the effect of permanent sunlight and shade. The arrangement of the windows is a regular spacing on both fronts overlaid by a larger geometry of interlocking diamonds, a pattern that is taken up in the mullions of the steel framed windows.
These shapes are completed by matching screens which act as balcony and terrace railings. The window lintels are cost concrete in the from of logs, to acknowledge the park opposite. The diagonal splay on the corner supports balconies at first and second floor levels. The lower is a small square enclosed by full height railings in the Spanish manner, the upper a larger triangle off the living room. This floor has another balcony off the kitchen in the form of a conical seat suspended over the pavement. The steep pitched roof is covered in deep blue glazed pantiles and forms the studio space at the top. The east wall of the house curves round to allow light into the rear windows of the neighbouring building. The internal staircose follows this wall in one sweep up to the top with a landing at second floor. This is the principle generator of the internal plan form, which varies considerably from floor to floor.

roof

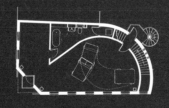
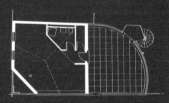
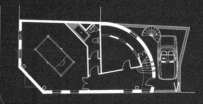
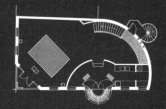

balcony

study room

bedroom

entrance

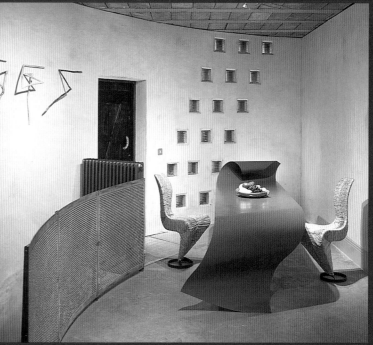
living room

genral facade

P : Offices
T : 200 Aztec West
D : C.Z.W.G.
C : Electricity Supply Nominees Ltd./Arlington
　　Business Parks Ltd.
L : 200 Aztec West, Almondsbury, Bristol
A : 12,670m²
M : Brickwork, Precast Cancrete, Aluminium,
　　Painted Plaster
photo by Jo Reid＋John Peck

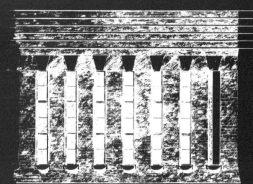

◎車がターンできるように正面玄関は円形に切られ、車で到着すると、ドラマの1シーンを思わせる。この円形は四角い中庭の建物の角に切られている。高い手摺とともに、雨どいといった田園的な特色より、むしろ建物に目盛りをつけたという印象をあたえる。荒涼としたアズテックの場所と公園の風景には異質に思える自動車をかくすために、各建物の中央に樹木におおわれた芝生の中庭をそなえる設計となった。

◎計画は2棟の同じ建物からなり、段階的に発展できるようにしてある。どの建物も280〜650㎡のオフィス・ユニットを入れることができる。それぞれが提供する貸オフィスの数や大きさは様々に変化し、これにより玄関のコンセプトがきまる。各オフィス・ユニットにはWC、身障者用WC、キッチン、ボイラー、空調室などからなるサービス・コアが完備している。

A vehicle turning circle generated the curved form of the main entrances giving some sense of drama to motorized arrival. These circles are carved into the corners of the square courtyard buildings and together with the use of a high parapet, give an impression of scale in the buildings rather than the rural idiom of the eaves gutter. To mitigate the weather-beaten Aztec site plus the dominance of the parked car over park landscape the design provides a sheltered lawned quadrangle with fruit trees in the centre of each building. The scheme consists of two identical buildings to allow for phased development. Each building can house a number of small office units ranging from 3000-7000 sq ft. The concept determines the entrances but allows a variation in the number and size of tenancies served by each. Each office unit may be seif-contained with service core comprising WCs, disabled WC, kitchens, boiler and electrics room with ducts for passible future air conditioning installation.

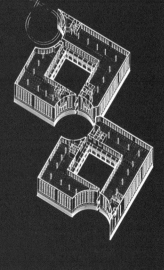

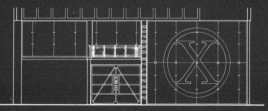

FRONT ELEVATION

LONGITUDINAL SECTION

facade

rear staircase

staircase detail

P : Apartment Block
T : China Wharf
D : C.Z.W.G.
C : Jacobs Island Co.Plc/Harry Neal Plc
L : London
A : 380m$^2$
M : Steel, Concrete, Painted Render

◎チャイナ・ウォーフは３つのマニエリスムス式ファサードをもつ。ミル・ストリートに臨む正面はスタイルの点で、以前倉庫だった近隣の建物に最も近い。煉瓦積みにより開いている窓は中央の狭間の開口部に向かって、サイズが小さくなっている。このにせの遠近法的効果はひとつには開口部の大きさを強調し、ひとつには、近隣の建物の異なる窓とに格差をつけている。それは内部のベッドルームからバスルームへの移行を十二分に表す。狭間の開口部自体は細長い１階の床で、ビルのサーキュレーション・エリアを表し、狭間は倉庫の運び上げサーキュレーションである。リフトと階段のサーキュレーション・エリアは隣に現在あるリード・ウォーフと共有であり、この珍しい関係は、そのビルが直接開口部に続くように見えることでよく分かる。

China wharf has three mannerist facades. The Mill Street elevation is the closest in style to its ex-warehouse neighbours. The window openings in the brickwork reduce in size towards the centre loophole frame opening. This false perspective effect partly emphasizes the openings' size and partly graduates between the different windows of the neighbouring buildings; it satisfactorily expresses the transition from bedroom to bathroom inside. The loophole opening itself is an elongated first floor and expresses the circulation area of the building, the loophole being the hoisting circulation of a warehouse . This circulation area of lift and stairs is shared by the existing Reeds Wharf next door and this unusual relationship is shown in the way that the building appears to run right into the opening.

riverside facade

entrance

entrance lobby

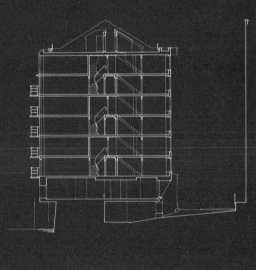

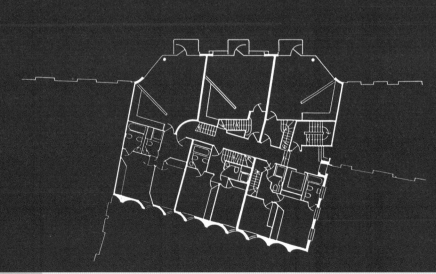

street entrance

◎この計画のコンセプトは川へと下っていく通行自由な通りまたは遊歩道に関してであり、計画の奥まった所から川を眺めるためである。現場はその眺めに向かってゆるい下り坂となっていて、建物の中のアパートからばかりでなく、歩道からもそれを楽しむことができる。区域全体は公共の歩行者用街路がＴ字に交差して、計画の中心でフープと呼ばれる半円形の大きなスペースになっている。
◎建築的に、波止場地域にあるその建物群はその地に２つの方法で応えている。現存する街路に面する敷地の縁の周りには、ロンドン・ストック・ブリックのファサードが近くの復旧された倉庫ビルディング群の高さによく合い、後者の重々しい力強さに、だき柱のある深い窓、ピラミッド型のバルコニーおよび大きなバットレスで応じている。

P : Office and Shop
T : Jacobs Island
D : C.Z.W.G.
C : Jacobs Island Co.,Plc.
L : London
A : 14,400m$^2$
M : Terazzo Blocks, Self Coloured Render, Steel, Concrete, Asphalt, Bricks, Georgian Wired Glass, Yorkstone, Granite

The concept of the scheme is of open streets or malls running down to the river to give views of the water from deep back into the scheme. The site is sloped down towards the view so that it may be enjoyed not only from the apartments in the buildings, but also at pavement level. The whole area becomes a criss-cross of public pedestrian streets culminating in a large semicircular space at the centre of the scheme to be called The Hoop. Architecturally the building respond to their Dockland location in two ways. Around the edges of the site on the existing streets, London Stock Brick facades match the height of the neighbouring fine restored warehouse buildings, responding to the massive strength of the latter with deep revel windows, pyramid balconies and large buttresses.

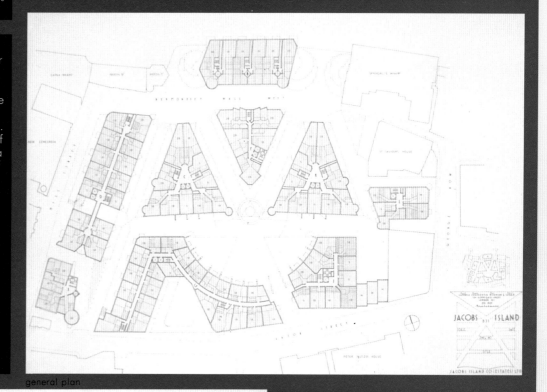

general plan

from Bermondsey

from the river

# CASSON MANN DESIGNERS
## カッソン・マン・デザイナーズ

P : Office
T : Charted Society of Designers Headquarters
D : Dinah Casson＋Roger Mann
C : Chartered Society of Designers
L : London
A : 600m²
M : Sand Blasted Steel, Stainless, Etched Glass, Copper, Lacewood, Ash, Bird's Eye Maple, Oak, Wenge, Merbau, Linoleum
photo by Peter Cook＋Richard Davies

◎このプロジェクトのデザイン意図は、既存のグレート1にリストされた建物と、パートナーシップによりデザインされた現代的備品と調度品の間に明白な区別をつけ、旧と新の間に幸せな結合ができるようにすることにあった。

The design intention of this project was to drow a clear distinction between the existing grade one listed building and the modern fixtures and fittings designed by the partnership, such that a happy marriage could be established between the old and new.

administration office

bar panels

front reception

library

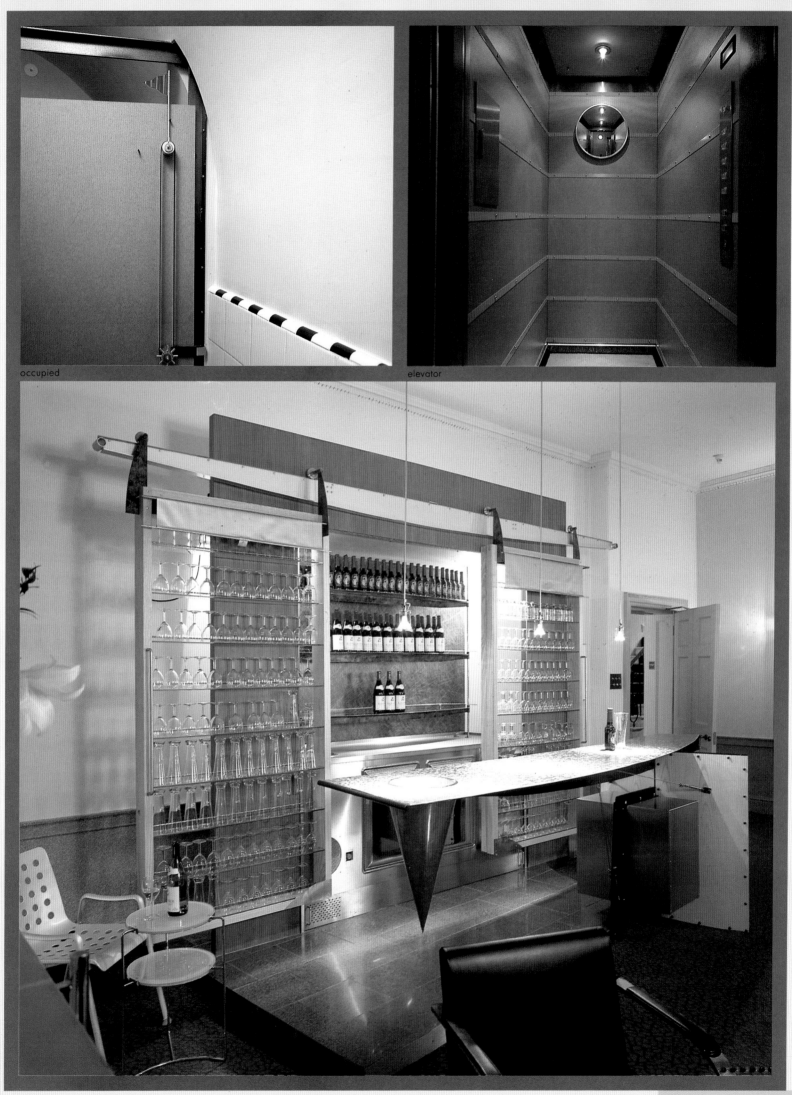

occupied

elevator

P : Studio Apartment
T : Roof/Studio Conversion
D : Dinah Casson＋Rpger Mann
C : David and Sue Pearce
L : London
A : 60m²
M : Colour Coated Aluminium, Stainless Steel,
     Polycarbonate, Bird's Eye Mapla
photo by David Pearce

◎重要なことは、あからさまに現代的でありなが
ら、ビクトリア朝に特有な様式の本質的な精神を
保つ新しい屋根の景観をつくりだすことであった。
近隣のマンサード・タイプの屋根の広がりは全く
感受性に欠けている。お互いに強めあうコントラ
ストを生みだす現代性を十分確信せず、それらの
屋根はアルミニウム・グレージングの長い水平な
線で、破風とドーマー・ウインドーで切れ切れの
ルーフ・ラインを埋めてしまって、テラスの質を
ぶち壊している。2階建の家に急勾配の屋根をの
せるのもまた極めてトップ・ヘビーな効果を与え
るものである。

The concern was to create a new
roofscape that was unashamedly
contemporary whilst keeping the essential
spirit of the Victorian vernacular.
Neighbouring Mansard-type roof
extensions are wholly insensitive. Not
sufficiently confident in their modernity to
create a mutually strengthening contrast
they destroy the quality of the terrace by
infilling the broken roofline of gables and
dormer windows with long horizontal
lines of aluminium glazing. The effect of
the steep slope on a two-storey house is
also very top heavy.

from Cedars road

skylight

lounge

# COOK＋HAWLEY ARCHITECTS
## クック＋ホーレイ・アーキテクツ

P : City Development
T : Way out West
D : Architects Peter Cook＋Christine Hawley
L : Berlin

◎ クルフュアシュテンダムのウエスト・エンドを
活性化するプロジェクトが設計された。段階的な
開発が行われることになった。
◎ 第一はアメリカンスタイルの格子状市街を計画
し、摩天楼を建てる。
◎ そのあとで一見軽いものが芽生えのようにニョ
キニョキ出始める。この「サボテン」様のものは
しだいに、自力で立つ建築物となり、景観の大半
を占めてしまう。
◎ 結局できあがった変わり種は、半ば植物、半ば
寄生物、半ば機械、半ば通常の建築物である。

A project designed to liven up the West
end of the Kurfurstendamm. It develops in
stages.
The first is the setting-up of an
American-style grid city: complete with
skyscraper.
Later some apparently casual growth-like
objects arrive and begin to sprout. These
'Cactus' objects gradually become an
architecture in their own right, taking over
much of the scene.
The eventual mutant is part-vegetable,
part parasite, part machine, part regular
architecture.

tree

detail

plan

lightweight strctures

tree

Berlin square

Berlin square

WAY OUT WEST : BERLIN SECTION B-B (RIG

AT STAGE 'D'　　0　　　　　　　　　　　　　　　50M　　　　　　PETER COOK 1988

P : Museum
T : The glass museum
D : Peter Cook＋Christine Hawley
C : The city of Langen, W Germany
M : Aluminium Faced, Glass and Steel Sheds

◎記念物としてのヨーロッパの博物館ではなくて、アメリカの美術品格納庫の伝統にのっとり、一連の光りを通さないギャラリーがガラスの斜面で結ばれてできている。北側は平穏で神秘的、南側は開けて、生気に溢れている。現代ステンド・グラスのコレクションは、そのためにこの建物が設計されたわけだが、この層の中心的役割を演じなければならない。

In the tradition of the American art shed, rather than the European museum as monument. Consists of a series of light tight galleries, linked by a glass ramp. The northern side is calm and mysterious, the south is open and exuberant, The collection of modern stained glass for which it is designed, must act as a central part of this layering.

from above

model

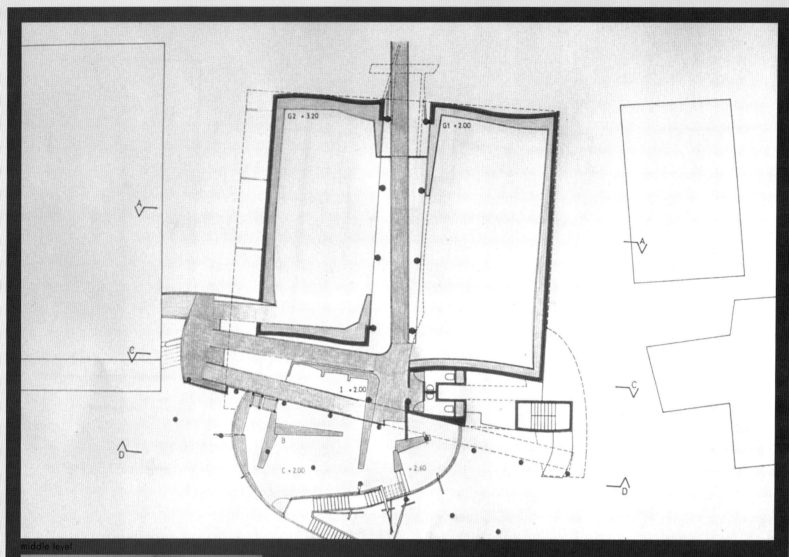

middle level

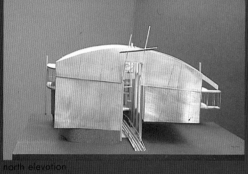

north elevation

site plan

ANSICHT

south elevation

OSTANSICHT

east elevation

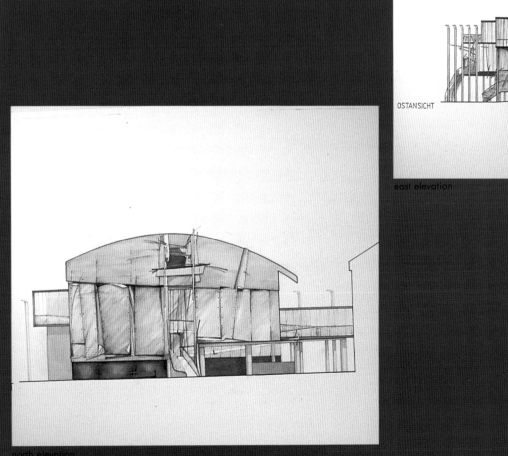

north elevation

P : City Development
T : Real City
D : Cook＋Hawley Architects
L : Frankfurt

◎オッフェンバッハの町と（他の周囲を取巻く別々の町を）結び合わせようとする市街拡張のプロジェクト。

◎広い「大通り」がつくられ、それに沿って「ヴィラ」が建つ。

◎各ヴィラはリフトと非常通路を入れる巨大なフレームである。これらは必要になるまで入居がないままで立っていて、最も早い時期の大通りのヘロイズムをつくりだす。

◎そのあと、それらは様々なタイプの建築によって「おおわれる」。間に合わせの、カサバみたいなものが生長する。

A project for the extension of the City so as to link up with the town of Offenbach (and other surrounding separate towns). Broad 'Avnues' are established, flanked by 'Villas'.
Each villa is a giant frame of lifts and fire corridors. These can stand unfilled by housing until needed, thereby creating the Heroism of the avenue in the earliest stages.
Then they are 'clothed' by a variety of types of architecture: Temporary, Kasbah-like, vegetated etc.

planting

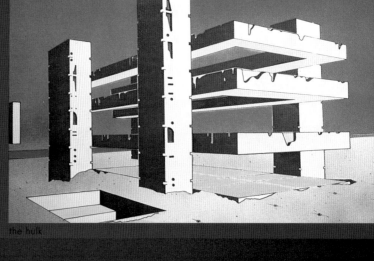

the hulk

with minimal additions

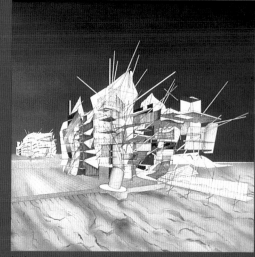

tents

layered screens

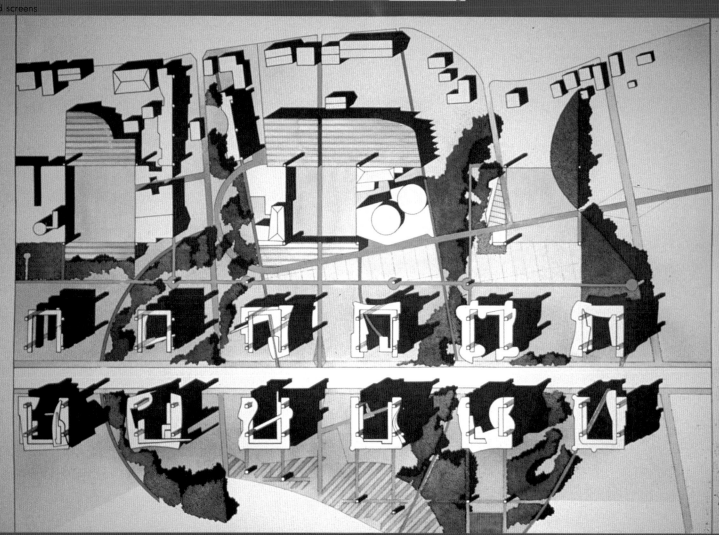

oberrad district plan

P : Arts Complex
T : Wettbewerb St Pauli Landungsbrucken/
    Millerntor
D : Cook＋Hawley with Herron Associates
C : City of Hamburg
L : Hamburg
A : Area in square metres n/a
M : Steel, Glass

◎ ホテル会議センター、博物館と展覧センター、ミュージック・ホール、ミュージック・フェスティヴァル複合施設、すべてが埠頭に沿って計画され、ハンブルクのドックを生き返らせるためのコンペティション摘要に応えて設計された。

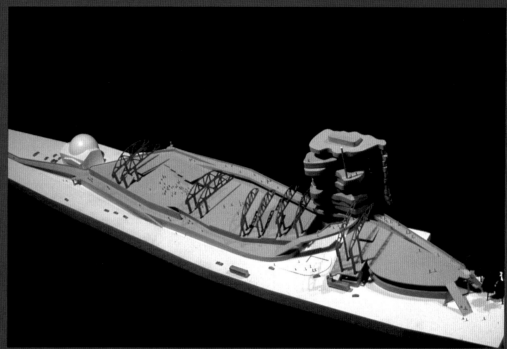
riverside pavilion

Hotel conference centre, museum and exhibition centre, music bowl, music festival complex, all planned along a land pier, designed in response to a competition brief for the revitalization of Hamburg's docks.

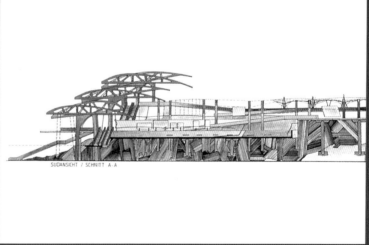
Cliff museum

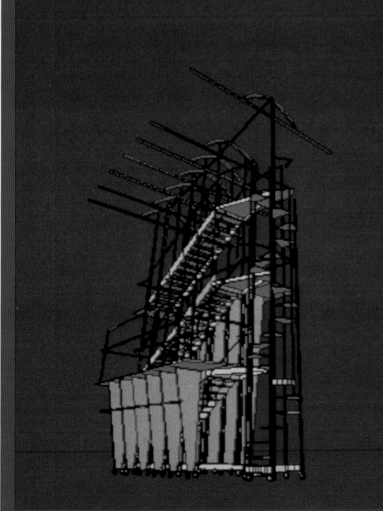
Nagoya yatai

P : Housing
T : Housing at Lutzowplatz
D : Peter Cook＋Christine Hawley
C : IBA Berlin
L : W.Berlin

◎「IBA」プログラムのための13戸のアパートメン
　トと2軒のショップ。ジキル博士とハイド氏的建
　物。東（コートヤード）側は静かで朝日のため窓
　を小さくする。洗面やベッドルームなど。
◎西側は開いて、少々クレージーで、おおっぴら
　である。時には高さが倍もあり、家族の団らんの
　場で、公園や景色を眺めわたせる。
◎アパートメントには隅や割れ目がふんだんにあ
　る。13戸のうちに9種のバリエーションがあり、
　あきさせない。

Thirteen apartments and two shops for
the 'IBA' programme.
A Jekyll and Hyde building, so the east
(courtyard) side is calm and
small-windowed for morning sun, shaving,
bedrooms, etc.
The west is open, a little crazy, overt,
sometimes double-height, it is where the
family gathers, looking out to the park
and the view.
Apartments are full of nooks and
crannies. Nine variations in thirteen. No
boredom.

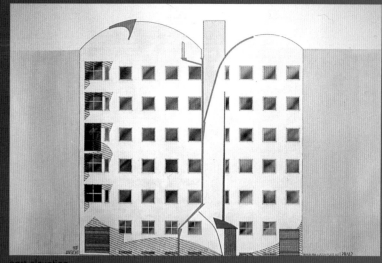

east elevation

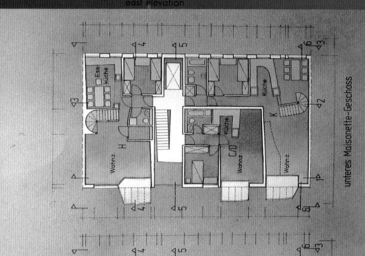

typical floor plan

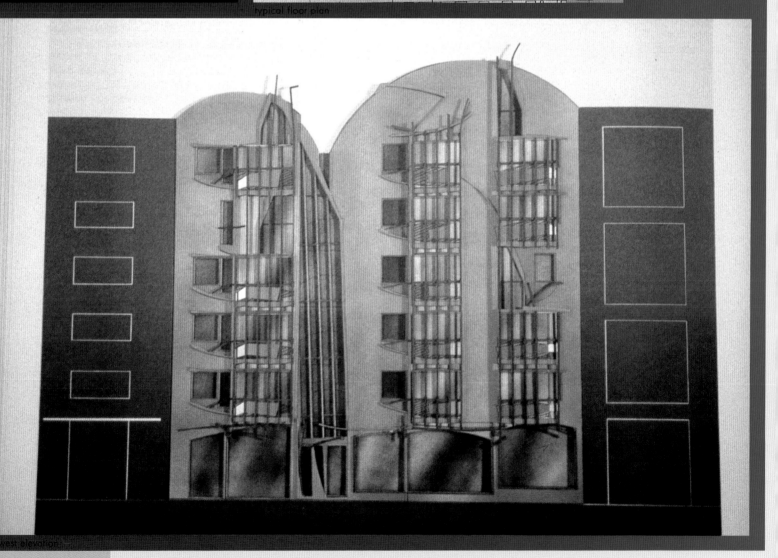

west elevation

# DANIEL WEIL+GERARD TAYLOR
## ダニエル・ワイル＋ジェラルド・テーラー

P : Domestic Residence
T : Domestic Residence
D : Daniel Weil＋Gerard Taylor
C : Peter and Mimi Buckley
L : London
A : 160m²
M : Floors: Lime Treated American White Oak,
    Carpets Wails Painted Plaster/Lighting: Low
    Voltage Recessed Lighting. Design by
    Arnold Chan, Isometric Ltd/Fixtures: Painted
    Timber, Maple, Beech, Alpi Veneers.
photo by Richard Davies

bedroom storage

bathroom

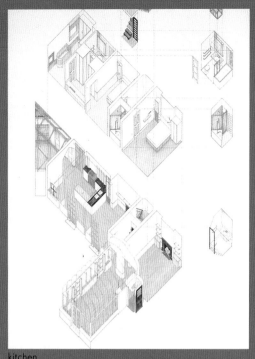

kitchen

living room

window shutters

P : Retail Shop
T : 'The Base', Retail Store
D : Daniel Weil + Gerard Taylor
C : French Connection
L : London
A : 255m²
M : Floor: Baltic Pine, Cpncrete/Walls: Breeze
    Blocks, Plaster, Paint Wash/Lighting:
    Special Fluorescent, Tungsten Bulb Fittings/
    Fixtures: Douglas Fir Wood, Galvanized
    Metal, Laminate
photo by Richard Davies

cafe

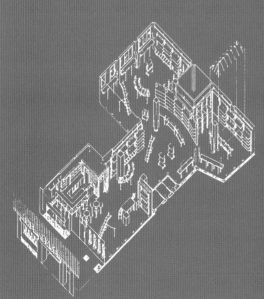

fitting room

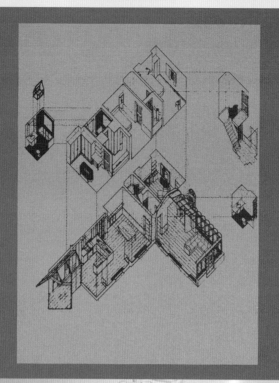

display shelves

rear of shop

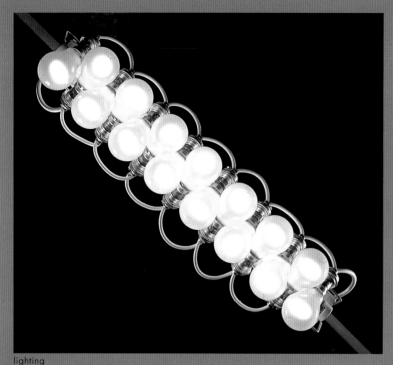

lighting

shop front

# DAVID CHIPPERFIELD + PARTNERS
## ディヴィッド・チッパーフィールド＋パートナーズ

P : Design Studio
T : Brownlow Mews
D : David Chipperfield + Parthers
C : Carroll, Dempsey and Thirkell
L : London
A : 1,400m²
M : Sandblasted Glass, Mirror, Marble, Steel,
    Plaster, Elm
photo by Richard Bryant

◎キャロル、デンシーとサーケルらは、ロンドンにデザイン会社をかまえることになり、デザインの優秀性をそこに反映させたいと願っていた。
◎湾曲したニレ材とスチールの壁に挟まれた大きな階段の玄関、スチールをさし込み、彫刻を施した手摺のある可動式のスクリーンに導かれ2階へいく。2階の施設は、デザイン・スタジオ、中庭を見わたす応接室、後部につながるスタッフの部屋と会議室からなっている。
◎建物の中央は以前製陶用の窯であったが、化粧室に改造された。そこへはスチールの階段をつけてある。これらの区域はカラー・フレームにすりガラスまたは鏡のパネルをつけたもので囲まれており、入口のパネルには白い大理石が一面にはってある。

Carroll, Dempsey and Thirkell are a successful graphic design company who wished to acquire a headquarters in London which would reflect the design excellence on which the firm's reputation is based.
A grand staircase entrance between a curved elm and steel wall and a floating plaster screen with an inset steel and carved marble handrail leads to the accomodation on the second floor, this comprises of a design studio and reception overlooking the mews lanc with partners suite and conference room to the rear.
The centre of the building was formerly a pottery ovens and has been converted into the toilets. These are readched by steps of folded steel sheet. These areas are enclosed by painted steel frames filled with panels of sandblasted glass or mirrors. The entrance panel is filled with white marble.

handrail detail

entrance

first floor plan

detail

reception desk

entrance to office

P : Gallery
T : Arnolfini Gallery
D : David Chipperfield＋Partners
C : Arnolfini Gallery
L : Bristol
A : 450m$^2$
M : Plaster, Portland Stone, Slate, Elm, Steel
    Terrazzo
photo by Peter Cook

◎ディヴィッド・チッパーフィールド＋パートナーズはアルノルフィニ・ギャラリーを刷新するために招かれた。そのプロジェクトにはエントランス・ホールの再設計とギャラリーのレイアウトの再編成が含まれた。レストランとバーがマルチ・メデア・アーチストのブルース・マクリーンとの協力で設計された。プラスター、ポートランド石、黒スレートおよびエルムといった天然の素材が使用され、２つのエレメント、レセプション・デスク（グリーンのラッカー仕上げ）と赤い階段のカーペットが、これらといい対照をなしている。レストランのシェルはギャラリーの美学を継続して使用し、これを背景に一連の彫刻が並べられて、バーはおもにスチールとテラゾでつくられている。

David Chipperfield and Partners were invited to renovate the Arnolfini Gallery. The project involved redesigning the entrance hall and re-organizing the layout of the galleries. The restaurant and bar was designed in collaboration with the multi-media artist Bruce McLean. Natural materials of plaster, portland stone, black slate and elm were used, and two elements stand in contrast to these, the reception desk (green lacquer finish) and a red staircase carpet. The shell of the restaurant continues the aesthetics of the gallery but set against this are a series of sculptural objects, primarily the bar constructed in steel and terrazzo.

entrance

bar

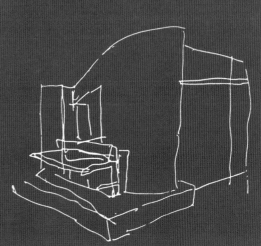

second floor plan

first floor plan

staircase

bar

lobby

# DAVID DAVIES ASSOCIATES
## ディヴィッド・ディヴィス・アソシエーツ

P : Office, Showroom
T : Valentino Headquarters
D : David Davies Associates
C : Valentino
L : Roma
A : 3,250m²
M : Marble, Chrome, Bronze, Westmorland, Slate, Maple, Lacewood, Frosted Glass

◎ DDAが採用したアプローチは優雅な簡潔さで、周囲の豊かさを申し分なく引立て、なおかつぜいたくな素材を使うことによって周囲の豊かさとも調和している。各面は慎重に設計され、その絶頂として新しいヴァレンチノの独特な本部ができ上がった。

The approach adopted throughout by DDA is one of elegant simplicity, providing a perfect, foil to the opulence of the surroundings, yet echoing these through the use of rich materials. Each aspect has been designed with care, culminating in the creation of a distinctive headquarters for a new Valentino.

reception area

entrance hallway

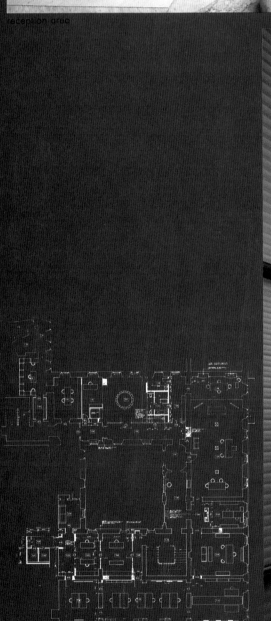

conference room

P : Shop
T : Valentino Paris(Re-Style)
D : David Davies Associates
C : Valintino
L : Paris
M : Marble, Chrome, Glass, Lacewood

◎顧客はまずウインドーの湾曲したグラス・ロッドのスクリーンのきらめきを背景にディスプレーされたコレクションに目をやる。ボカドル通りのエントランスはドラマチックな、高さが倍もある大理石のホールへ通じる。大理石ダストの壁をめぐらし、きらめくクロームの円盤で華麗さを増している。

◎裁縫室の中は、コレクションが壁を埋め、回転するガラスのスクリーンの背後に、ぜいたくな品々が展示されている。特別にデザインされたラグ、ソファ、アクセサリー・キャビネットがスペースを満たしている。

◎部屋は湾曲したアクセサリー壁によって、円柱が並び、3枚の背の高い鏡と毛足の長い、優美なラグで効果を増しているギャラリーと結ばれている。湾曲した壁は、グラス・ロッドの大きくゆるやかなカーブからつくられたキャッシュ・デスクを際立たせ、婦人物と紳士物のコレクションを分かつ、自然で、きわめて重要なポイントの役をつとめる。

◎ここでは、卵形の円柱がアメリカスズカケ材のパネルの華かさと単純な大理石の床を背景に立ち並ぶ。2個のアメリカスズカケ材のキャビネットが、広々としたエントランス・ホールへの入口となり、ホールはアベニュー・モンテーニュとアンパス・デュ・テアトルの角に向かって開いている。

Clients first glimpse the collections displayed against the sparkle of curved glass rod screens in the window. The rue du Bocador entrance leads into a dramatic, double height marbled hall, lined with marble dust walls and enriched with sparkling chrome discs.
Inside the couture rooms, the collections line the walls, with luxury items displayed behind pivoting glass screens. Specially designed rugs, sofas and accessory cabinets complete the space.
The room is linked by a curving accessory wall to a column lined gallery enhanced by three tall mirrors and a long, elegant rug. The curved wall features a cash desk formed out of a sweeping curve of glass rods, acting as a natural pivotal point between the ladies' and men's collections.
Here, over columns are set against the richness of lacewood panels and the simple marble floor. Two lacewood cabinets form a gateway into the spacious entrance hall, which opens out onto Avenue Montaigne and the corner of Impasse du Theatre.

couture room

P : Shop
T : Oliver-Rome
D : David Davies Associates
C : Valentino
L : Roma
A : 2,000m²
M : Bronze, Black Walnut, Maple, Satin Chrome, Glass, Westmoreland Slate, Marble

◎オリヴァはクチュール・ハウス、ヴァレンチノが若いスタイル・コンシャスな個人に訴えるためにつくった、新しいファッション・ラベルである。
◎DDAは新しいコレクションを収容する小売環境をつくってほしいと依頼された。ローマ店は現在国際的に拡張されているチェーンの本店である。
◎ローマの中心、ヴィア・バブイノにあるかつてアート・ギャラリーであった18世紀の建物をDDAは慎重に改造し、3つのファッション・ルームにした。そこでは伝統的なデザインと現代のデザインを注意深く融合させている。

Oliver is a new fashion label created by the couture house Valentino to appeal to the younger style-conscious individual.
DDA were approached to create a retail environment to house the new collection, and the Rome shop is the flagship of a chain that is now being expanded internationally.
Situated in Via Babuino in the heart of Rome, DDA have sympathetically converted this Eighteenth Century former art gallery into three fashion rooms which carefull blend traditional and contemporary design.

video wall & balustrade

mannequin

archway to rear

# DIN ASSOCIATES
ディン・アソシエーツ

P : Shop
T : Next Department Store
D : Rasshied Din
C : Next Retail Plc.
L : Kensington High Street
A : 930m$^2$
M : Brass, Inlayed Terrazzo, Oak, Beech
    Kevasingo, American Cherry, Ceramic Tiles,
    Slate, Stainless Steel Silver Epoxy
photo by John O'brien

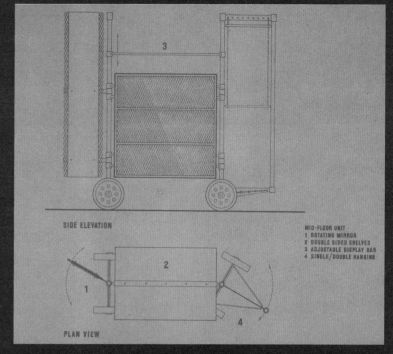

◎ デパート X は店舗デザインにおいて革命的なコンセプトをもつものである。はじめて小売環境における保管と検索を機械化し、保管区域から衣服を取り寄せる新しいシステムを採用し、お客が衣服を手にするまでの時間を短縮した。検索システムの全体が眺められ、お客は希望の衣服が上の階からくるのを見ることができる。試着室は保管システムの前にあり、動くレールに向かって開かれている。

◎ 自動化されたウインドー・ディスプレーと幅 5 m、高さ 4 m の回転ドアがあり、ドアの重さは2.5 t である。

◎ この店は若い旅行者をターゲットに絞り、視覚的な効果を狙っている。全体のコンセプトはショッピングにおける興奮をテーマにしている。

Department X is a revolutionary concept in store design utilising for the first time in a retail environment a totally new mechanized storage and retrieval system to allow garments to be called up from the stock and storage areas, thus cutting out the usual waiting periods for garments to arrive.
The whole of the retrieval systems are on display customers can see their garments arriving from the floors above. Fitting rooms are positioned in front of the moving storage systems and are open onto the moving rails.
There is a robotized window displays and a 5m wide by 4m high pivoting front door which weighs 2 ½ Tons.
The store is aimed at a younger tourist audience and is very visual, the total concept brings excitement back to shopping.

revolving & door

facade

revolving carousel

**GROUND FLOOR PLAN**
14 STAIRS
15 TWO-STOREY PATERNOSTER
16 OXFORD STREET
17 CENTRALLY PIVOTED DOOR
18 VIDEO WALL
19 MENS CHANGING CUBICLES
20 MEN'S WEAR CAROUSEL
21 MENS WEAR COUNTER
22 STEEL TILED FLOOR AREA
23 WINDOW DISPLAY CAROUSEL

dispenser & trolleys

café

FRONT ELEVATION

SECTION

PLAN VIEW

2

1

3

MERCHANDISE SYSTEM
1 PRIMARY FRAME -
  ADJUSTABLE HANGING
2 SECONDARY MOVING FRAME -
  ADJUSTABLE SHELVES
3 FITTING ROOM

clothes railing detail

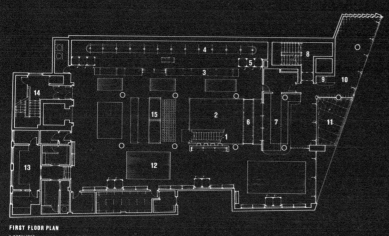

**FIRST FLOOR PLAN**

1 ESCALATOR
2 VOID
3 LADIES' WEAR COUNTER
4 LADIES' WEAR CAROUSEL
5 LADIES' CHANGING CUBICLES
6 GLASS BRIDGE
7 SERVERY
8 FIRE EXIT AND STAIRS
9 CASH DESK
10 INDOOR CAFÉ AREA
11 GLAZED CAFÉ TERRACE
12 LADIES' WEAR DEPARTMENTS
13 GENERAL OFFICES
14 STAIRS
15 TWO-STOREY PATERNOSTER

walk way & mobile

P : Shop
T : Next Department Store
D : Din Associates
C : Next retail Plc.
L : London
A : 930m²
M : Brass Inlayed Terrazzo, Oak, Beech
    Kevasingo, American Cherry, Ceramic Tiles
    Slate, Stainless Steel, Sliver Epoxy
photo by Peter Cook

身長大の窓ガラスを使っているので、店の正面から店のレイアウトが部分的に見える。スペースと人の劇的な効果は巨大なステージに似ている。こうした劇場と意外性の要素は店全体に拡張されて、そこでは「全体の眺め」が垣間見られ興味深い見通しへと移り変わっていく。このようなスペースの計画は顧客の気をそそって、探検の気分を満喫させてくれる。この発想は、いつも先へ進む楽しみを生みだしてくれた英国の庭園の伝統からである。

By using full height glazing the store's frontage allows a sectional view into the shop,s layout. The dramatic effect of space and people is not unlike an enormous stage.
This element of theatre and surprise is extended throughout the store, where a 'total view' is replaced by glimpses and interesting vistas. The planning of these spaces encourage the customer to enjoy a sense of exploration, the inspiration for this came from the English garden tradition which has always created a feeling of progression and delight.

clock

shop front

mixed daylight

shop center

staircase

electronic partitioning

P : Shop
T : Next The Jewellers
D : Din Associates
C : Next Retail Plc.
L : London
M : Inland Marcatre, Cast Aluminium, Stainless
    Steel, Patinated Bronze, Terrazzo Curved
    Glass, Dark Hardwood, Persian Rugs
photo by Peter Cook

◎プランはゆっくり収斂するレンズの焦点にもとづく。レイアウトは顧客の気をそそって店に招き入れ、気のむくままにゆっくり客に眺めてもらえるようにデザインされた。
◎商品の配置は最大限に店の中が見られるようになっていて、正面のファッション宝石類は柔かくカーブしたカウンターに展示され、自然と「高価な」商品へと流れつくようになっている。
◎インテリアは宝石細工師の技術の複雑さからインスピレーションを得ている。象眼したマルカルトル、鋳造アルミニウム、ステンレス・スチールおよび緑青をふいたブロンズのような素材を用いて、表面材の質感と細部におおいに注意が払われている。

The plan is based on the gently converging focal points of a lens. The layout has been designed to encourage the customer to enter the shop and browse at will. The merchandise is positioned to allow maximum visibility into the shop, the fashion jewellery at the front is displayed on soft curving counters which flow naturally into the 'precious' areas. The interior derives inspiration from the intricacies of the jewellers craft. Great attention has been placed on the surface texture and detail by using such materials as inlaid marcartre, cast aluminium, stainless steel and patinated bronze.

shop front

showcase

display cabinet

LONGITUDINAL SECTION

TYPICAL FLOOR PLAN

1 WINDOW DISPLAY
2 FASHION JEWELLERY COUNTER
3 CASH DESK
4 FASHION JEWELLERY WALL
5 LIGHTING CANOPY
6 WATCH DISPLAY CASE
7 PRECIOUS JEWELLERY COUNTER
8 STAFF AREAS

# D'SOTO '88 DESIGN GROUP
## デ・ソト '88 デザイン・グループ

P : Brasserie
T : Blakes Brasserie
D : D'Soto '88
C : Derrick Blake, Sammy Teshuve, Blakes
    Brasserie Ltd.
L : London
A : 200m²
M : Green Slate, Black Terrazzo, Glazed
    Plaster, Metal, Timber Floors, Fumed Oak
    Bar

◎建物のいろいろなエリアの相互の関係から、処理にいくつかのロジスティックに導き出された選択が生まれた。これらの場合、建築上の制約のあるところでは、デ・ソトは素材の仕上げと家具によって強調することに決めた。予算の大部分を、最も重要な構造の、そしてサービス部門の工事につぎこまねばならなかったことにより、課された制約内で、仕上げは慎重に選ばれた。デ・ソトは天然の素材に対する熱情を、いつも興味深いやり方、たとえば表面仕上げや塗料加工を避けるなどで強調してきた。この建物はグリーンのスレートと黒のテラゾのような素材を、グレイの光滑剤をかけたプラスターの壁、古色を帯びさせた金属、天然の木材の床、および煙でいぶしたオークのバー設備と家具に並置させて、この方針の実例となっている。金属を用いたところはすべて腐食から守るため、磨いてクリア・ラッカーをかけている。照明は全体にシウ・ケーイ・カンから供給された低圧の設備を使って控え目で簡素なものにした。ただひとつ譲歩してぜいたくにしたのものは、SKKのリモートコントロール「ロボット照明」である。
◎家具は本質的な形と合理的、幾何学的な形との、在来の型にとらわれない並置、および使われた素材の処理法の両方において、その企画を補完するように、デザインされた。

basement detail

The relationships of the various areas of the building to one another created a number of logistically derived choices of treatment. In these cases, where they were constrained architecturally, D'Soto decided to allow the finishes of the materials and the furniture to create an emphasis. The finishes were carefully chosen within the constraints imposed by the large proportion of the budget which had to be devoted to essential structural and services works. D'Soto has always emphasized its enthusiasm for natural materials expressed in interesting ways, with an avoidance of applied finishes and paints, and the building is an example of this philosophy, with materials such as green slate and black terrazzo being juxtaposed with grey glazed plaster walls, aged metal/natural timber floors and fumigated oak bar fittings dend furniture. All metalwork was polished and clear lacquered as a protection against corrosion. Lighting was kept discreet and simple, with low voltage fittings throughout supplied by Shiu Kay Kan, the only concession to extravagance being one of SKK's remote control "robotic lights"

main bar

The furniture was designed to complement the scheme both in its unconventional juxtaposition of organic and rational geometric forms, and in its treatment of the materials involved.

general view

staircase

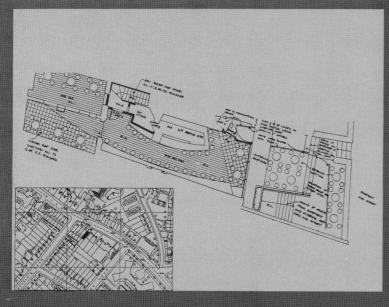

rear conservatory room

rear conservatory room

P : Shop
T : Boyd and Storey
D : D'Soto '88
C : Helen Storey, Karen Boyd, Amalgamated Talent
L : London
M : Polished Steel, Copper, Used Pine, Grey Slate Tile Flooring
A : 80m²

◎ 店のイメージはジュール・ヴェルヌのメカニックとビクトリア朝の技術をそのスペースに適合するよう縮少してやわらげた、現代風再解釈であった。備品の形とスペースの計画は「ニュー・スピリット」デザインを実践したもので、型にとらわれず、それでいて機能的な形が、様々な天然材によって表現された。上述の可動備品が店のレイアウトに、重要な役割をはたしていて、スペースは額面以上に利用されている。たとえば客がいないときは、可動式の席は旋回させて平たくたたみ、壁に寄せて置くことができる。

The imagery of the shop was a modern re-interpretation of Jules Verne's mechanics and the world of Victorian engineering, scaled down and softened up to suit the space. The shapes of the fittings and the planning of the space was an exercise in "New Spirit" design, where unconventional yet functional forms were expressed in a variety of natural materials. The aforementioned moveable fittings play an important role in the layout of the shop, where space is at a premium. For instance the changing cubicle swivels and folds flat against the wall when there are no customers.

jewellery cabinet

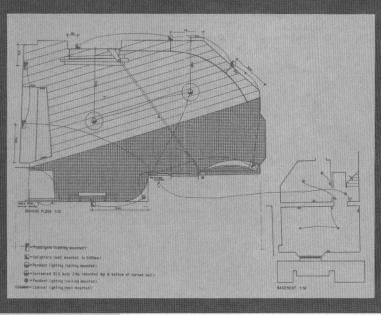

moveable sign

railfitting & changing room

moveable railfitting

# EVA JIRICNA ARCHITECTS
## エヴァ・ジリクナ・アーキテクツ

P : Shop
T : Joseph
D : Eva Jiricna Architects
C : Joseph Ltd.
L : London
A : 1,000m²
M : Spanish Marble, Plaster, Fibrous Plaster,
　　Stained Cherry, Polished Stainless Steel,
　　Sand Blasted Glass
photo by Peter Cook

rear of shop

◎ 建築家たちが依頼されたのは、紳士服、婦人服、アクセサリーに家具などからなる様々な部門をもつ「ミニ・デパートメント・ストア」のデザインを用意することだったが、この段階で特定されていなかった。店はロンドンのファッション・ウィークである1988年10月までに開店する予定だった。
◎ 初期の打合せで、ジョーゼフは「エイリーン・グレイをミックスしたイタリア風の宮殿」の雰囲気を提案した。正式のレベルでは、この店の扱いにくいジオメトリーを組織して秩序と焦点を生みだし、他方で十分な試着室とスタッフや収納のエリアを用意することが必要であった。利用できるスペースを広げるため、既存のオフィス、貯納室およびターンテーブルは取り除かれ、新しいショップ・ウインドーがスローン・アベニューに面してつくられ、プランの最も奥に日光を入れた。中央の軸がつくられ、そこに階段が置かれ、再編成された後の壁に取りつけられた身長大の鏡が最高の効果となっている。

downwards view

The architects were asked to prepare designs for a 'mini department store' to include a variety of departments, consisting of menswear, womenswear, accessories and furniture but at this stage unspecific. The shop was to be open by 1st October 1988 being London fashion week.
During early discussions Joseph mentioned the atmosphere of 'an Italian palazzo mixed with Elleen Grey'. On a formal level it was necessary to organize the awkward geometry of the shop to create order and a focus whilst maximizing the retail space and providing sufficient fitting rooms and staff and stock areas. To enlarge the available space the existing offices, store room and turntable were removed and a new shop window formed on Sloane Avenue to obtain daylight into the deepest part of the plan. A central axis formed onto which the staircase has been relocated, culminating in a full height mirror on a realigned back wall.

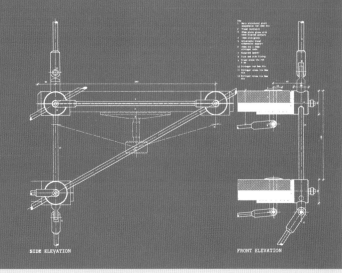

SIDE ELEVATION　　　FRONT ELEVATION

shop front

staircase

hangrail

behind stairs

staircase

display shelves

gallery

P : Nightclub
T : Legends
D : Eva Jiricna Architects
C : K.T.Ltd.
L : London
M : Travertine Marble, Aluminium, Stainid
    Maple, Stainless Steel
photo by Alistair Hunter

◎依頼者の予算内にとどめるため、構造の変更は最小限にする必要があった。デザインは現存の不規則で組織だっていない。三層のスペースを統一し、1階のレストランとキッチン、現存の中2階レベルを通って、地下レベルのダンス・フロアと化粧室にサービスするサーキュレーションを合理化することにあった。デザインの中核としての新しい階段を入れたため、全体の詳細図をつくるのに、ひとつのテーマを提供することになっている。

In order to keep within the client's budget it was necessary to minimize the structural alterations. The design unifies the existing irregular, uncoordinated spaces on three levels and rationalizes the circulation to serve the restaurant and kitchen on the first floor, dance floor and lavatories on the basement level via an existing mezzanine level. The insertion of a new staircase as a core to the design provides a theme for the detailing throughout.

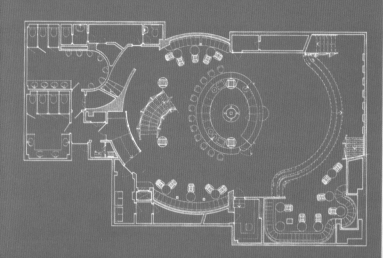

downstairs bar

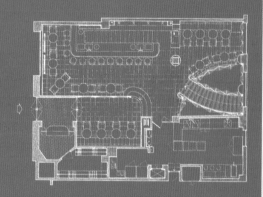

central staircase

bar

P : Apartment
T : Flat 2, Royal Victoria Patriotic Building
D : Eva Jiricna Architects
C : Private Client
L : London
A : 260m$^2$
M : Maple Flooring, Mild Stainless Steel, Tensile Cable, Paited Plaster
photo by John Donat

balcony

◎南ロンドンにあるビクトリア朝の会館内で、260m²のルーフ・スペースを2人のミュージシャンのために改造する。
◎摘要として、バスと鏡台つき洗面台を室内に設置したベッドルーム2つをつくり、残りのスペースをオープンにして、キッチンとユーティリティ・エリアを囲ったエリアとして加えるだけにした。
◎容積を最大限に利用するため、屋根を支える既存の木材の真束トラスを外して、その代わりにルーフ面の勾配にぴったり沿うケーブル構造にした。

Conversion of a 260m$^2$ roof space for two musicians within a Victorian institutional building in South London. The brief was to provide two bedrooms, both with bath and vanitory stations sited within the rooms and to leave the remainder of the space open plan, with only a kitchen and utility area as additional enclosed areas.
Maximum use of the volume was achieved by moving the existing timber king post trusses supporting the roof and replacing them with a cable structure which closely follows the pitch of the roof plane.

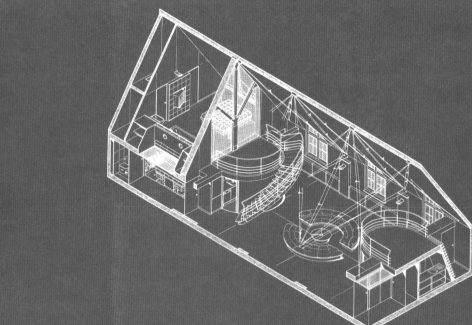
lounge

kitchen

staircase

P : Offices
T : Vitra Building
D : Eva Jiricna Architects
C : Vitra
L : Birsfenden
M : Glazed Walls, Aluminium Panels, Concrete
Filled, Steel Tubes, Steel Castings, Steel
Ceiling Beams

◎ 高度制限の敷地規制のため、プロジェクトは4棟の独立した4階建の建物が中央のサーキュレーション・コアで連結されるというデザインにもとづいている。

◎ 街路に面した前面は垂直に立ち上がるが、反対側は低層の被いのついたアトリウム・スペースのある中央コートヤードに向かって開いている（風景の要素をもって展示の目的や、スタッフの食堂に利用される）。段を上がって、小さな植物などをあしらったバルコニーと、下のレベルにできるかぎりの大きさのオフィス・フロアをつくりだしている。

◎ 日光を最大限に取り入れるためと、建物が平均以上の奥行をもつことから、身長大の窓が考えられ、環境条件は垂直のライト・ウェルを入れたことで改善されている。ライト・ウェルは、光を別にして、中央スペースに新鮮な空気を供給する。

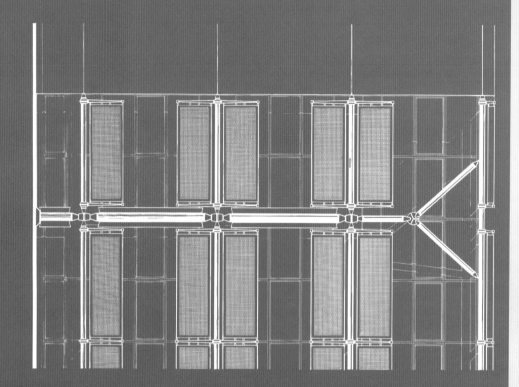

Due to height limitations and site restrictions the project is based on a design of 4 individual 4 storey buildings linked together by a central cirulation core.

The street elevation goes up vertically while the other side opens into a central courtyard with low level covered atrium space (to be used for exhibition purposes and staff canteen with landscape element), and steps up producing a little landscaped balcony and maximum achievable width of the office floor on the lower levels.

Full height windows are considered to give the maximum amount of light and due to the more than average depth of the building, the environmental conditions are improved by the introduction of vertical light wells which, apart from light, supply the central space with fresh air.

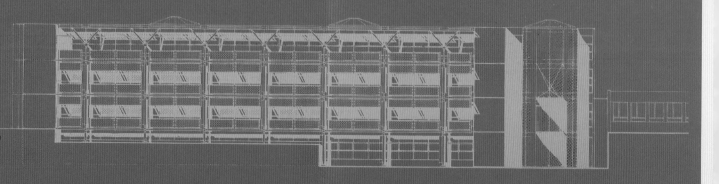

south elevation

# FISHER PARK LTD.
## フィッシャー・パーク・リミテッド

P : Stage Design
T : Nelson Mandela 70th Birthday Tribute
D : Fisher Park
C : Elephant House Production
L : Wembley Staium, London
A : 60m Wide/50m Walkway
M : Paintings, Starvision TV Screens

◎ネルソン・マンデラの70歳の誕生日を祝ってコンサートが催された。コンサートのテーマは、アパルトヘイトに反対する作品で国際的に有名な6人の画家によって表現された。これらは、アリーナの正面とステージを飾るのに用いられた。ステージの装飾は別のシーンのために変化させることができた。メイン・ステージの脇にＴＶ・スクリーン・ヴィジョンが立てられ、パフォーマンスを中継したり、映画などを上映した。第２ステージはメイン・ステージの切替え中に、演奏用として使用された。12の主なロック・バンドと他にも多くのアーチストが10時間におよぶコンサートに参加した。演奏の装置は４台の10ｍ×６ｍの移動プラットフォームにしつらえられ、パフォーマンスの幕間にステージの上を移動した。

The concert celebrated the 70th birthday of Nelson Mandela.
The theme of the concert was illustrated by specially commissioned paintings from six artists internationally known for their work opposing Apartheid. These pictures and other key images were enlarged and used to decorate the arena frontage and stage. The decorations on stage could be changed to produce different scenes. The main stage was flanked by starvision TV screens which relayed performances and presented specially commissioned films.
The second stage was used to present performers during the changeovers on the main stage.
Twelve major Rock bands and many other artists played during the 10 hour concert. Band equipment was set up on four 10x6m rolling platforms which were moved on and off the stage between performances.

Annie Lennox

Annie Lennox

stage

P : Club
T : The Hippodrome
D : Fisher Park
C : Peter Stringfellow
L : Leicester Square, London
M : Stainless Steel, Black Steel,
    Silver Anodized Aluminium,
    Computerized lighting,
    Laser and Mechanical effect

◎このクラブは前舞台のアーチとひな段式の座席
のもつ劇場を改造したものである。クラブは昼と
夜で別々の機能をもっている。昼は会議やファッ
ションショーなどの会場となり、夜はライブ演奏
の設備をもつディスコとなる。7個の衛星がダン
ス・フロアを照らす照明効果となっている。衛星
は照明パネルを閉じて天井に収納される。ダンス
・フロアから3mの高さまで下げることができ、
パネルを開きダンス・フロアの上に、光とネオン
の六角形の天井を形づくる。衛星はコンピュータ
制御され、様々に変化する。
◎照明、レーザー、ビデオおよびクラブ内の機械
類はすべてDJコンソールからコンピュータによ
って制御されている。ビデオスクリーンにより、
自動プログラムを実行させ、事前に機能を選択し、
確認することができる。

The club was converted from an existing
theatre with a proscenium arch and tiered
seating. The club supports separate
functions during the day and the night. In
the day it is a venue for conferences,
fashion shows etc., at night it is a
discotheque with facilities for live
performances.
The seven satellites provide the major
effects lighting over the dance floor. They
are stored in the roof with the lighting
panels closed. They can be lowered to a
height of 3 metres above the dance floor
and the panels can be opened out to form
a hexagonal ceiling of light and neon
over the dance floor. Each satellite can be
positioned under computer control at
various heights with the panels various
inclinations.
All the lighting, laser, video and
mechanical functions in the club are
controlled by computer from the DJ
consol. LED mimic arrays and video
screens allow all the functions to be
preselected and previewed as well as set
to run on automatic programmes.

general view

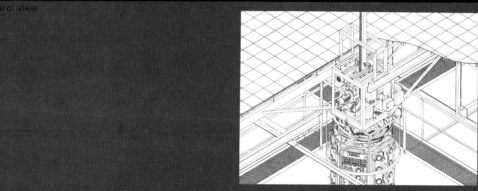

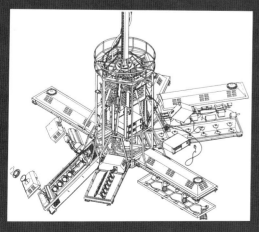

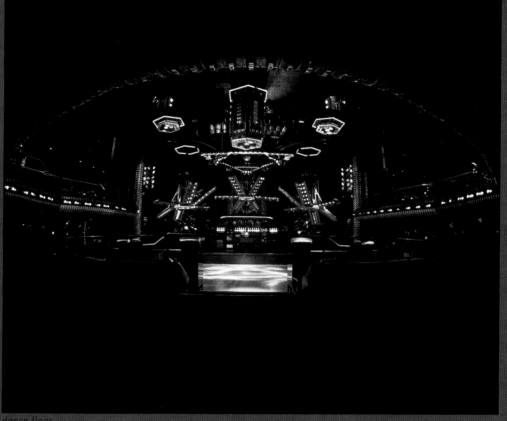

dance floor

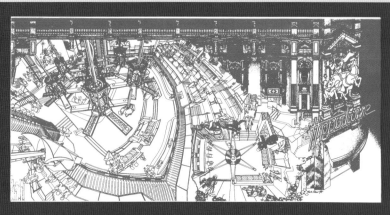

satelites

balcony

satelites

view from stage

central satelite

view from stage

P : Stage/Concert Platform
T : Faith
D : Fisher Park
C : George Michael
L : Japan, Australia, USA and Europe
M : Fire Retardant Fabric, PVC, Lighting, Laser,
    Thin Wall Aluminium Tube

◎ セットはステージを取囲むアルミニウム・バーのケージからつくられた。ヴァリライツとカラレイがケージの内側の面につけられた。ケージの正面と側面はコンサート中パッと開き、終ると同時に閉じる。

◎ ステージ全体はロゴマークのついたカーテンで三方をとり囲まれた。聴衆にケージを見せるためカーテンは持ち上げられ、コンサートが終ると下ろされた。

The set was created from a cage of aluminium bars which enclosed the stage. Variloites and Colorays wrer mounted on the inside faces of the cage. The front and sides of the cage swung open during the concert, and closed simultaneously at the end.
The whole stage.was enclosed by a three sided curtain carrying the FAITH logo. The curtain was raised to reveal the cage to the audience, and lowered at the end of the concert.

cage

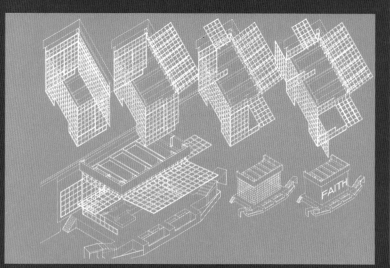

open cage

stage risers

P : Stage/Concert Platform
T : The Wall, Performed Live
D : Fisher Park
C : The Pink Floyd
L : Los Angeles, New York, Dortmund and London
M : High Strength aluminium Alloy, Glass Reinforced Plastic, Honeycomb Panelling Cardboard, Inflated PVC

stage bomber

◎ショーを考え、指導したのは、ピンク・フロイドのリード・シンガーで作曲家のロージャー・ウォーターズであった。アート・デレクターは、英国の諷刺漫画家、ジェラルド・スカーフだった。ショーはあるロック・スターの誕生から、名声、富を得て、恥ずべき行為をなし、贖罪に到る、不安にさいなまれた一生を描いた。
◎ショーは聴衆席の端から端までのびる、白煉瓦の壊れた壁を通して見えるステージから始まった。壁は幅60m以上で両側で高さが10mあった。壁の中のギャップはコンサートの前半中、裏方が入って、順次バンドをかくした。第2部の大半、バンドは映写スクリーンとして使われた壁の後にあり、見えなかった。それはショーの終わりの合図と同時に崩れ落ちた。

The show was conceived and directed by Roger Waters, lead singer and composer of the Pink Floyd. The art director was Gerald Scarfe, the English satirical cartoonist. The show portrayed the angst ridden life of a rock and roll star from birth through fame, fortune, and ignominy to redemption.
The show opened with the stage visible through a deconstructed wall of white bricks which stretched from one side of the auditorium to the other. The wall was over 60m wide and rose to a height of 10m on either side. The gap in the wall was filled in by stage hands during the first half of the concert, gradually concealing the band. For most of the second half the band were invisible behind the wall which was used a projection screen. It collapsed on cue at the end of the show.

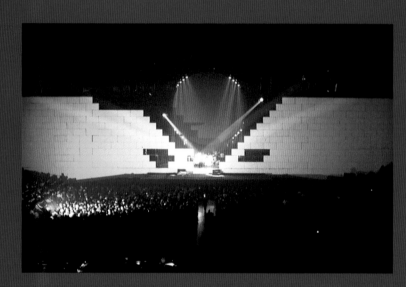

equipment assembly

Roger Waters

equipment

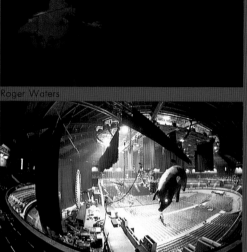
inflated pig

lighting trusses

filming the wall

collapsing wall

wall equipment

P : Stage/Concert Platform
T : The Pro's and Con's of Hich-hiking
D : Fisher Park
C : Roger Waters
L : Europe And USA
M : Scenery Gauze, Aluminium Trussing

◎ コンサートの夢の世界はモーテルのベッドルームの内側で上演された。ベッドルームをつくりだしている背景はショーを通じて、ワイド・スクリーンと交替した。映画のイメージがTVに、またはモーテルの窓を通して、またはスクリーン全体に映して聴衆に提供された。映画はニック・ローグ指揮のライブ・アクションとジェラルド・スカーフが描き監督する、アニメーションの合成からできていた。

The dreamworld of the concert was presented inside a motel bedroom. The scenery which created the bedroom alternated with the wide screen throughout the show. The film images were presented to the audience either on the TV or through the window of the motel, or across the whole screen. The film consisted of a mixture of live action, directed by Nick Rog, and animation drawn and directed by Gerald Scarfe.

animation

film projection

motel room table

close-up

puppet on catwalk

# FOSTER ASSOCIATES
## フォスター・アソシエーツ

P : Shop
T : Esprit
D : Foster Associates
C : Esprit/Joseph
L : London
M : Sand Blasted Float Glass, Stainless Steel,
    Painted Mild Steel, Concrete
photo by Richard Bryant

◎ イングランドのエスプリはジョセフと提携した。ロンドンのスローン・ストリートにある最初の店は、やはりフォスター・アソシエーツが1978年にジョセフのため設計した店を引き継いだものである。角地のためフロアースペースが狭い三角形となるので、このベースメントを活用して、物理的、視覚的にも拡張することが、設計上の課題となった。しかし、店が2つの階に展開した場合、下の階が見劣りして孤立してしまう問題があった。新しいデザイン・コンセプトはガラスの階段を中心とする単一の垂直的なスペースをつくりだすことにした。グリップラストの垂直なスチールの支柱と、表面が樺の軽いパネルを使い、陳列と収納をフロアーの縁に押しやった。このために設計されたシステムにより、インテリア・ディスプレーが自由に変えられるようになり、大規模なウインドー・ディスプレーが可能となった。店を劇場に見立てれば、ここでは衣服が演技をし、メッセージを伝えている。自然な仕上げ、粗打ちのコンクリート、無着色の金属と木材は、自由に変更できる照明システムとともに、適切な、そして何にでも調子を合せられる舞台装置である。

Esprit in England have teamed up with Joseph and their first shop in Sloane Street, London replaces an earlier shop also designed by Foster Associates for Joseph in 1978. The corner site generates a tight tringular floor space and the desigh challenge was to enlarge this both physically an visually by using the basement area. However, the traditional problem with two level shops is that the lower floor can become isolated as a second-grade space.

The new deigh concept dissolves this difference by creating a single vertical space centred around a glass staircase. Display and storage is pushed to the floor edges using vertical grip-blasted steel supprts and light birch faced panels. This system which was specially designed for the project allows total flexibility for interior display and large-scale window dressing. The shop is close in spirit to theatre, where the actors and the messages are, the clothes. In that sense the neutral range of natural finishes, raw concrete, unpained metal and timber together with a very flexible lighting system provide an appropriate and tuneable stageset.

basement

shelves

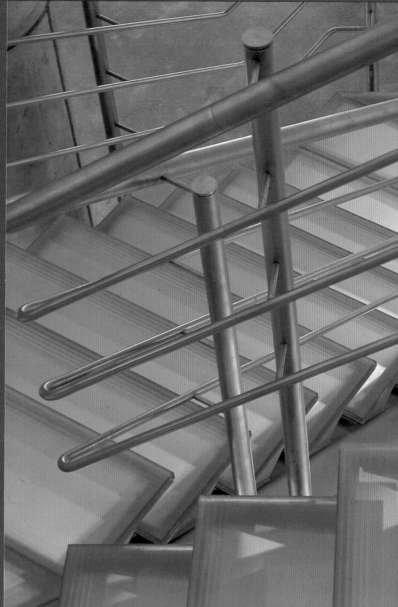

staircase well

sliding rail detail

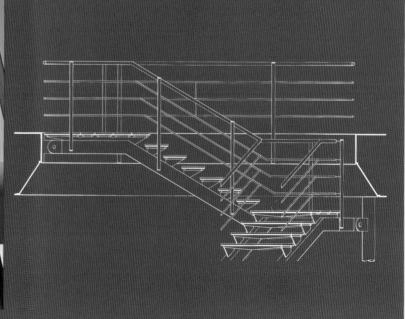

ladders on rubber wheels

P : Shop
T : Katherine Hamnett Shop
D : Foster Associates
C : Katherine Hamnett
L : London
M : White Glass, Mirror, Steel
photo by Richard Bryante

◎店舗のデザインにおいて、スペースが一方の重要関心事とすれば、照明——照明の質——がもうひとつの関心事である。スペースは側面からの光——古い工業製品の窓に透明で輝く白ガラスを入れ替える——と屋根の細長いガラス窓から入る直接のトップライトのコンビネーションにより生かされた。夜はルーフライトが外から点灯されて、やわらかな背景光線となり、通路の可動スポット・ライトがそれを補う。スポット・ライトはスペース全体にわたり構造的ジオメトリーを照しだす。
◎光とスペースの質、白を強調した仕上げとふんだんに使われている鏡は、バレエ学校か、衣服等のディスプレーのためのスタジオを思わせる。目標は、高価な、洗練された家具に頼らずに、時間を超越した質感をつくりだすことにあった。そうした家具を手に入れる時間も予算もなかったという事実は別として、率直にいってそれが適切であるとは感じられなかったのである。

If space is one preoccupation in the design of this shop then light — the quality of light — is the other. The space is brought to life by the combitation of side light — the old industrial windows reglazed with white glass glow with a translucent effect — and direct top light from strips of roof glazing. At night the roof lights are lit from outside and give a gentle background lithe supplemented by moveable spot lights on tracks whic pick up the structural geometry across the space.

The quality of light and space, predominately white finishes and generous use of mirrors, is evocative of a ballet school or studio to provide a complementary setting for the clothes and their display. The aim was also to create a more timeless quality that would not depend on expensive or sophisticated furniture — aside from the fact that there was neither time nor money to afford them — they were frankly not felt to be appropriate.

# KATHARINE HAMNETT

illuminated entrance

main shopfloor

full mirrors

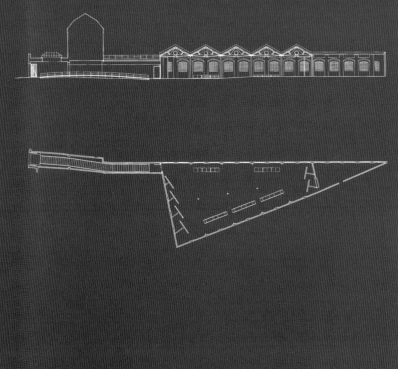

P : Art and Study Centre
T : Hediateque et Centre D'Art Contemporain
D : Foster Associates
C : Ville De Nimes
L : Nimes
photo by Richard Davies

from the street

◎1984年のコンペティションのあとニームのメディアテク・アンド・アートセンターの依頼を受け、フォスター・アソシエーツの最も難しいプロジェクトのひとつとなった。計画の建物は紀元前3世紀のローマ寺院に面し、この都市の伝統的な枠組ばかりでなく、この寺院に関連づけたものにしなければならなかった。
◎敷地は昔市立劇場があったところである。3つの案がだされた。そのひとつは残っている劇場のコロネードを組み入れる案である。4番目の案は、現在建設中だが、中心を外れたガレリアがあり、3つのおもなレベルで計画されている。1階にメディアテクがあり、ポンピドー・センターのように、本、レコード、映画、美術などを提供し、劇場と闘犬の切符売場もついている。その上の展示スペースは自然光で照らされる。1階の図書館フロアはルイス・カーンから借りた装置、光のシャワーにより照らされる。各階は内部では軽量スチール・ケーブルで吊された、コンクリート傾斜路により、外部とはガラスをはめたリフトと階段により結ばれている。

The Nimes mediatheque and art centre commission was won after a limited competition in 1984 and has proved to be one of Foster Associates most difficult projects. The proposed building faces a third century AD Roman temple, and has to relate to this as well as the traditional fabric of the city.
The site was once occupied by a municipal theatre. Three schemes have been proposed, including one which incorporated the surviving theatre colonnade. The fourth scheme. now under construction is planned on three main levels, with an off-centre galleria. The Mediatheque on the first floor, like the Pompidou Centre, provides books, records, film and art, together with booking offices for theatres and bull fighting. The exhibition space above is lit by natural light, the library floor at ground level lit by light funnels, a device borrowed from Louis Kahn. The floors are linked internally by concrete ramps. suspended by light steel cables, and externally by glazed lifts and staircases.

front facade

model

Roman temple

P : Telecommunications Tower
T : Barcelona tower
D : Foster Associates
L : Barcelona
photo by Richard Davies

◎バルセロナ・テレコミュニケーションズ・タワーのデザインは1988年6月のコンペティションで獲得された。その構造物はバルセロナ・オリンピック大会、マドリッドのワールド・カップおよび'92年の万国博に間にあうよう完成されるのだが、町を見おろす山頂の展望のきく場所を占める。タワーのデザインは最少の構造手段で最大限の効果を達成するというフォスターの哲学に従っている。出発点は小さな直径のシャフトだが、それは船のマストか旗竿を思わせ、プレカスト・コンクリートの部品からなっていて、ただひとつの基礎台にのっている。この核心部は120度ずつの間隔で置かれた3個のスチール製垂直トラスに固定され、全体の構造は山腹にしっかり固定されたポストテンション法を施した支え鋼につなぎとめられる。

Designs for the Barcelona telecommunications tower were won in a limited competition in July 1988. The structure, which will be completed in time for the Olympic Games in Barcelona, the World Cup in Madrid and Expo. 92 in Seville, will occupy a commanding position on a mountain top above the city. The disigh of the tower follows the Foster philosophy of achieving maximum effect with minimal structural means. The starting point is a narrow diameter shaft — echoing a ship's mast or a flag pole — made up of precast concrete components and resting on a single foundation pad. This core is braced by three vertical steel trusses set at 120 degrees to one another and the whole structure is tethered to post-tentioned guys anchored in the mountain side.

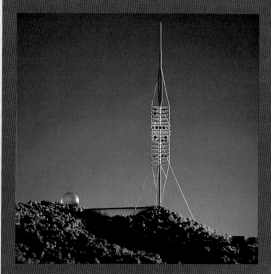

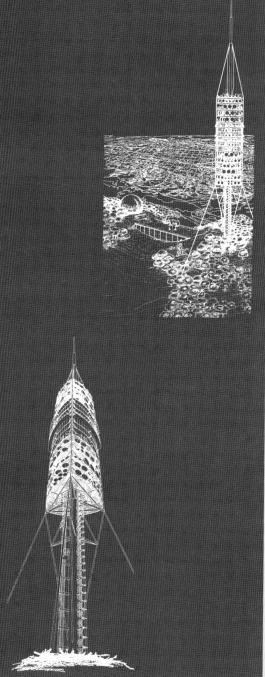

Barcelona tower

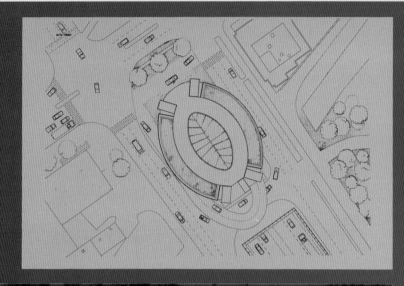

◎コンセプトはらせん形の駐車場を組み入れている。その形は敷地の周りの道路計画から生み出されて、その続きは上の長円形ホテルとなっている。24層の建物は高速道路をまたいで立ち、地上から7階上の構造上の移動レベル（またメイン・プラントも含む）からフリーウェイのヘリへ広がる8本のおもな円柱で支えられている。受付はエスカレーターで行くのだが、街路レベルの真上に浮かび、一段低いところにあるユトレヒツェバーンが見おろされ、長円形のアトリウムがドラマティックに建物の高さいっぱいまで立ち上がっている。駐車場のランプはアトリウムをらせん状に回り、受付を職務室および客室から隔てている。上部構造は分かれて、アトリウムを見せ、建物全体に光りをあたえ、透明にする。各階の両端にあるロビーからの眺めは壮観であり、他方カーブのついたファサードは周囲の公園用地への見晴らしを最大限に生かしている。

The concept incorporates a spiral car park, its shape generated by traffic planning around the site and its continuation forming the elliptical hotel above. The 24 level building straddles the motorway supported from a structural transfer level (which also houses the main plant) 7 floors above the ground by 8 main columns splayned back to the freeway edges. Guest reception, accessed by escalator, floats just above street level with the sunken Utrechtsebaan visible below and with an elliptical atrium rising dramatically above for the full height of the building. The car park ramps spiral around the atrium separating the reception from the hotel function rooms and guest rooms. The superstructure has been split to reveal the atrium and provide light and transparency through the building and allows spectacular views from lobbies at either end of each floor while the curved facades maximize views over the surrounding parkland.

model

highway

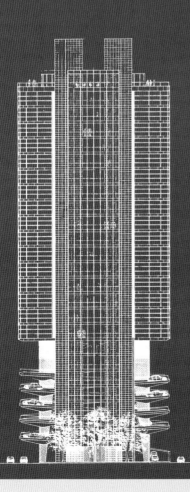

P : Underground Rakway
T : Bkbao Metro
D : Foster Associates
L : Bkbao
photo by Richard Davies

◎トンネルがプロジェクトのおもな要素で、洞窟群がトンネル工事に本来備わる形を明らかにしている。ステーション洞窟へは、エスカレーターの使用により、できるだけ簡単に、直に入っていくようにする。幅16mのステーション洞窟はスチールのシャッターを使い、現位置にコンクリートで建設する。細かいさねはぎ模様が建設ラインを表し、かつスケールとなる。インテリアのモデリングは人工照明と慎重なコントロールによって可能となる。システムのプレハブ部品（メザニン、階段、改札口、リフトなど）は主洞窟内の別々の要素とみなされ、ステンレス・スチールやガラスのような耐久性のある素材でつくられよう。プレハブ部品の滑かで洗練された品質は洞窟の壁のどっしりした重量感と対照をなしている。

The tunnel is te main element in the project and the caverns reveal the from inherent in tunnel engineering. Entry into the station cavern will be as simple and direct as possible by means of escalators. The 16 metre wide station caverns will be constructed in in-situ concrete using steel shutters. A fine pattern of rebates reflect construction lines and provide scale. Modelling of the interior is made possible by the careful control of artificial light. The prefabricated components of the system (mezzanines, stairs, ticket barriers, lifts, etc. ) are seen as separate elements within the main cavern and will be made of durable materials such as stainless steel and glass. The smooth and refined quality of the prefabricated components offer a striking contrast to the weight and solidity of the cavern wall.

tunnel section

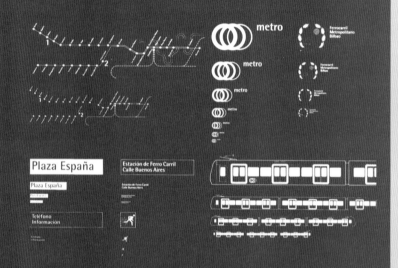

tunnel lining

# HERRON ASSOCIATES
ヘロン・アソシエーツ

P : Herron Associates, with Cook & Hawley
T : Wettbewerb St Pauli Landungsbrucken/
　　Millerntor
D : Herron Associates
C : City of Hamburg
L : Hamburg
M : Steel, Glass

◎曲りくねった埠頭の道の一部は公園予定地の樹木の梢を分けて通る。そこには収納可能なカバーやスクリーン、デッキおよびハンブルクの風の強い気候に応じた構造物が組み込まれる。埠頭に沿って立つ、ハイテクノロジーのミニ・パビリオンまたは小屋は、フェスティヴァルやスポーツ、コンサート、そして在来の公園のカフェ、バー、野外音楽堂に加えて、その他の娯楽施設のためのものである。
◎この企画の建物はイギリスの海岸保養地の伝統──今日のエレクトロニクスを駆使した軽量化された世界に出会っていたら、こんな風になったかもしれないという──を受け継いだものである。ハンブルク市の波止場地域は新しいヨーロッパ都市の原型……ことによるとロンドンの波止場地域のためのモデルとなる可能性をもっている。

Part of the route of the snaking land pier takes it through parkland treetops. It incorporates a sophisticated system of retractable covers and screens decks and fabric structures which respond to Hamburg's windy climate. High technology mini-pavillions or nodes along the land pier provide for fairs, sporting, concert, and entertainment facilities in addition to the cafes, bars and bandstands of the traditional park. The architecture of the scheme is a continuation of the English seaside tradition as it might have been — had it met up with the electronic and lightweight world of today. The docklands zone of the city of Hamburg has the possibility of becoming a prototype of the new European city......a model for London's docklands perhaps ?

hotel model

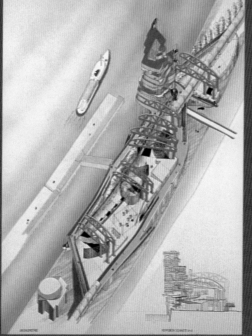

hotel elevation

Hamburg docks

computer mapping

FESTIVAL STRUKTUR (ENTFERNBAR)

FESTIVAL STRUKTUR (ENTFERNBAR) – GENUTZT

PLM 8B LANDPIER

Hamburg docks

hotel model

ANSICHT 1:20

BRÜCKENKONSTRUKTION

Hamburg docks elevation

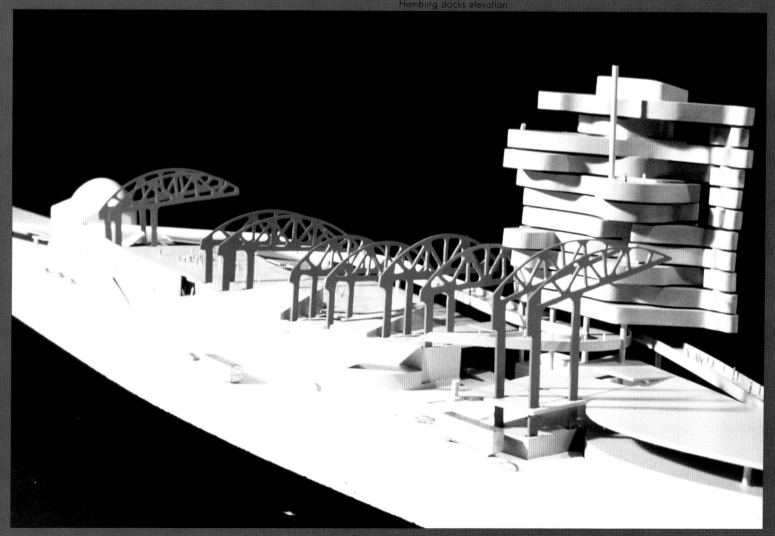

P : Office headquarters    L : Karlsruhe, W.Germany
T : L'Oreal Headquarters   M : Skeletal Glass Skin, Steel Hangers,
D : Herron Associates          Stretch-Form Blue Anodized Stainless Steel
C : L'Oreal

◎既存の市街と様々な会話をかわす4基のタワー。タワーが立つのは不等辺四辺形の隅で、それがなければ特徴のない既存の都市景観を明確に区切っている。

◎北部と西部へのルートはこの歩行者用カーペットがスペースの向うまで伸びていることを、視覚的に示唆している。課されている階層的な秩序は、渦巻き形に増大する尺度と、外から保護されている公共広場から東へ向かう幹線道路への移行の両方により示唆される。企画は3つの主要な活動の経営管理、製品、マーケッティングとヘア・ドレッシング学校について明確に打ちだした。それらは独立して活動するが、連絡は確保される。管理と製品の両部門は密接に結びついている。両者はガラスでおおわれた連絡ブリッジをもち、垂直のサーキュレーションとエントランス・パビリオンを共有する。このツイン・タワーは本部エレメントをなし、幹線ルートに隣接している。

◎理容学校は自律的に機能し、公共への出入りとして歩行者用専用ショッピング街路に向いている。両方のエントランス・パビリオンは上記のおもな構造つまり相互の関係を物語っている。対照的に、製品タワーの下には、パビリオンがロレアルからの独立を明白に表して立っている。この囲いの中には店が入り、広場の午後の陽だまりに面してカフェがある。独立を強調するため、サービス・ライザーは骨組のケージだけを残して外側を脱ぎ去って、そのコーナーをきれいにし、広場から覗き見られるようにしている。

Four towers, engage in a shifting conversation with the existing city fabric. The placement of the towers at the corners of the trapezium shaped site, defines the boundaries of an otherwise featureless extending urban landscape. The routes to the North and West extend this pedestrian carpet, suggesting a visual extension beyond the given space. An imposed hierarchical order is suggested by both the spiralling increase in scale and the shift from protected public square to the principle arterial route to the East. The program defined three principle activities management and administration, products, marketing and hairdressing school, which were to act independently but to remain connected. The admin and products department have close associations. They share the same verticle circulation and entrance pavilion, with cross circulation provided by glazed bridge links. These twin towers form the headquarters element and are adjacent to the arterial route.

The hair school operates autonomously, orientated onto the pedestrian shopping street for public accessibility. Both entrance pavilions engage the primary structures above, to illustrate their interrelationship. In contrast, under the products tower, the pavillion stands clear clarifying its independence from L,Oreal. This enclosure houses shops with a cafe facing onto the afternoon sun trap of the square. To accentuate this independence the service risers peel away leaving the structural cage to be exposed freeing the corner, allowing glimpsed views across the square.

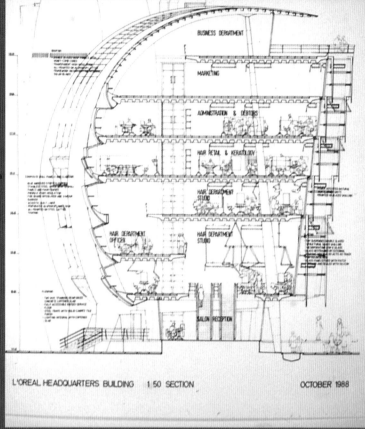

L'OREAL HEADQUARTERS BUILDING   1:50 SECTION          OCTOBER 1988

hair school

L'Oreal Headquarters

Keiser strasse

L'Oreal Headquarters

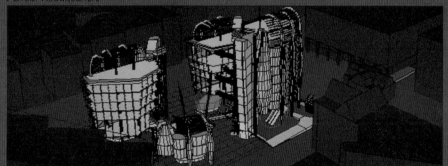

tower cluster

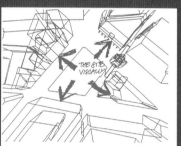

THE PLATZ VISUALLY EXTENDS BEYOND THE GIVEN SITE........TAKE ADVANTAGE OF THIS !!

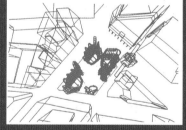

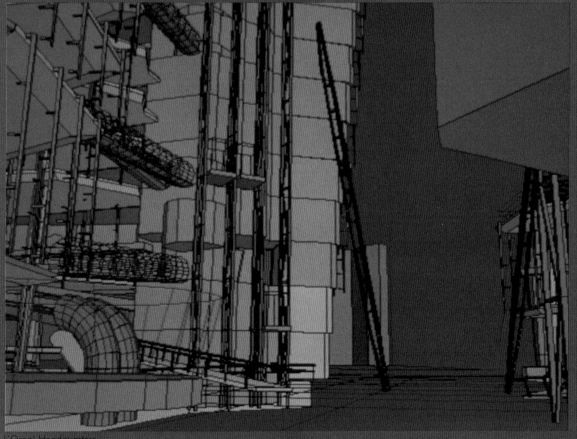

L'Oreal Headquarters

P : Office Headquarters
T : Store Street
D : Herron Associates
C : Imagination
L : London

◎このプロジェクトが当面する問題は、新しいオフィスに割当てられるインテリアの徹底的な改装のほかに、元来分離している2つのブロックを連結することと、建物と周囲のインターフェイスをつくりだすことにかかわっている。

◎ヘロン・アソシエーツはこのコートヤードを前と後の建物をつなぐブリッジウェイのシステムをもつ、広いオープン・スペースに設計した。中央スペースは一連の「フライング」スチール支柱に引っ張られた。やわらかい、白の半透明な屋根におおわれている。さらに屋根は折りたたまれ、建物の背部と側面をおおってテラスの屋根となり、両側を2つのガラス壁で閉ざされて、ギャラリーを形成する。

◎おおいのある通路のアイディアは、確かに新しくはないが、ここでは、コートヤードの高いレベルの歩道によってつくりだされた、破線のおもしろい図形的な遊びによるばかりでなく、以前からの建築物と競いあう能力によって形態上のバイタリティを取り戻している。

The problems faced in the project, besides the complete refurbishing of interiors to be allocated to the new offices, concern the connection of the two originally separate blocks, and the creation of an interface between the building and its surrondings.
Herron Associates have designed the courtyard as a broad open space, with a system of bridgeways connecting the front and back buildings. The central space is covered by a soft white translucent roof, tensioned by a series of "flying" steel struts. The roofing furthermore folds over the back and sides of the construction to cover a terrace, closed on either side two glazed to form a gallery.
The idea of the covered passage, certainly not new, is however given a renewed formal vitality here by its capacity to compete with the previous architecture, as well as by the interesting geometric play of broken lines created by the high level walkways in the courtyard.

computer model

imagination building

gallery

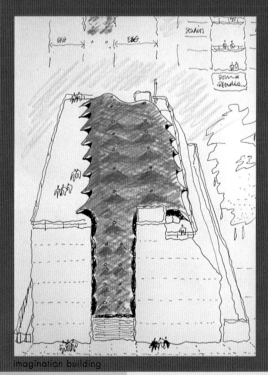
imagination building

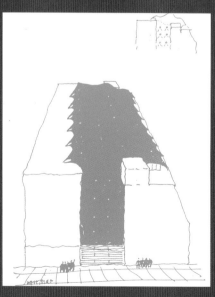

# IAN RITCHIE
## イアン·リチー

P : House
T : Eagle Rock House
D : Ian Ritchie Architects
C : Ursula Colahan
L : Near Uckfield, East Sussex
A : 235m²
M : Tubular Steel, Perforated Aluminium,
    Woven PVC, Aluminium/Steel Frames,
    Sandstone/Carborundum Sheet, Insulated
    Plyboard
photo by Jocelyne Van den Bossche

from the rear

◎この家は連続するスペースにおけるひとつの試みとして方向づけられていた。その図形、光りと影によるその抑揚においてである。
◎クライアントのはっきりした望みは、家の構成と、その結果である敷地のトポロジーや植物との対話を伝えることにより、鳥の特徴をもたせるという考えであった。考えは、構造の相互関連と翼の宙吊りによって実際の形に表現されている。尾はガラスの温室として把捉され、中で保護されている植物がオークやセイヨウヒイラギや砂岩からなる自然の景観に対照的な要素となっている。外側のブラインドの動きは気候に合わせて羽毛を立てる鳥の動きを演じ、ロフト·スペース（鳥の頭部）はこの家のインテリジェント·フォーカスで、かつエネルギー·センターである。
◎設計は外部の表面の処理において、最初のコンセプトと異なっている。最初は彫像と考えて、面、構造そして接合部は原色で表現された（リエトヴェルト·チェア）が、このアイデアは秋の色の微妙なコンビネーションを使うカモフラージュ的なものに進歩し、庭園と建物の間に垂直な造園用メッシュをはることによって、さらに壁の固い面を溶融させて、見晴らしを連続させて内部と外部を結びつけるガラスの開口部だけを残している。
◎この家の名は敷地の北縁に露出している岩に由来する。そのシルエットがワシを思わせるのである。ワシ岩は地方の測量地図に載っており、歴史的な連続性をもつ情緒的なエレメントを提供している。

This house has been directed as an essay in sequential space; its geometry, and its modulation by light and shade.
The notion of avian characteristics informing the composition of the house and the consequent dialogue with the topography and flora of the site, was an expressed desire of the client. The translation is realized thuogh the articulation of structure and suspension of wings; the tail as a trapped crystal greenhouse with its protected plants playing counerpoint to the natural landscape of oaks, holly and sandstone; the movement of external blinds as a play on the ruffling of the bird's feathers in response to the climate; and the loft space (bird's head) the intelligent focus and energy centre of the house.
The desigh differs from its original concept in the treatment of external surfaces. Originally conceived as a sculpture whose planes, structure and joints were articulated in primary colours (Rietveld chair), this idea evolved into one of camouflage using a subtle combination of Autumn colours and by applying vertical landscape meshes between the garden and building, attempting to further dissolve the solid planes of the walls leaving only glass openings through which internal and external spaces are linked by a continuous vista.
The house derives its name from an outcrop of rock at the Northern edge of the site, the silhouette of which is reminiscent of an Eagle. The name Eagle Rock is recorded on a local survey map and provides an emotive element of historic continuity.

entrance

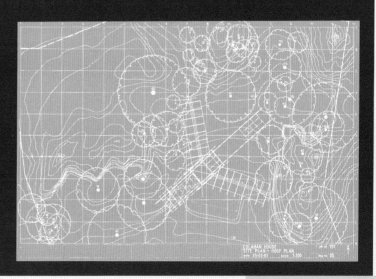

living area

rear door

general view

P : Greenhouse
T : La Villette
D : Ian Ritchie Architects
C : Establissement Publique, Parc de La villette.
L : Paris
A : 6,150m²
M : Cast Stainless Steel Tubes and Connections, Toughened Glass, Stainless Steel Cable/ Tension Rods
photo by Jocelyne Van Den Bossche, Alain Guisdard, Guy Deshayes

◎新しい科学技術産業博物館の南側ファサードの「3つの公共の窓」を代表して、中心をなすコンセプトは博物館と公園の両方から見て、透明さというコンセプトを確立することであった。

◎これは表面全体をおおうガラスのフラッシュ・カーテンをつくることにより、またこの表面に固定点を置くことによって達成された。これらの点は透明であることを表現するとともに、ガラスを互に固定させ、その結果構造を支えている。

◎各温室は高さ32m、幅32m、奥行8m（10階建の建物に相当する）である。おもな構造は8m×8mの格子で2m×2mのガラス16枚がこの構造格子にはまっている。

◎つくりだされたスペースは博物館を公園に結びつけ、博物館自体のショップ・ウインドーとなるよう、視覚的に活用されるはずである。中央の温室はすでに造園されて、やがて放電を縦続接続するリングを入れることになる。

Representing the "Three Public Windows" on the South facade of the new Museum of Science Technology and Industry, the central concept was to establish the notion of transparency, viewed both from the Museum and the Park.
This was achieved by creating a flush curtain of glass over the entire surface and by placing solid points in this surface. These points make the transparency readable, and are the fixings of the glass to each other and subseqently back to the structure.
Each greenhouse is 32m high, 32m wide and 8m deep (equivalent to a 10 storey building). The main structure is on a grid of 8m x 8m, and the 16 sheets of glass 2m x 2m occupy this structural grid.
The spaces created are to be exploited visually to relate the Museum to the Park, and to be a shop window for the Museum itself. The central greenhouse has already been landscaped and will eventually include a cascading ring of electrical discharge.

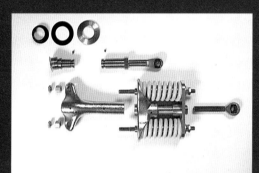
glass fixing.

greenhouse.

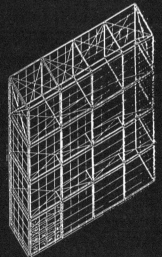
glass wall.

P : Entrance Hall Roof
T : La Villette Roof
D : Ian Ritchie Architects
C : Establissement Publique, Parc de la Villette
L : Paris
A : 2,400m², 2×250m² Domes
M : Roof: Teflon Coated Fibreglass/
    Dome: Laminated and Toughened Glass
    with Aluminium
photo by Jocelyne Van Den Bossche, Alain
Guisdard, Guy Deshayes

domes

◎科学技術産業博物館の中央ルーフは博物館に入る天頂の光線のヒエラルキーを確立し、エントランス・ホールのルーフの方形のエリアをはっきりと、幾何学的に分割するように考えられた。

◎これはそれぞれ直径18mの回転ドーム2基を置くことで達成された。ドームはロボット操縦の鏡が入っており、断熱で通風性の二重になったテフロン組織で、光を通し、新しい3Dルーフに収められている。

◎テフロン・ルーフは入射光の約2％を通し、下のスペースのために、光のヒエラルキーのベースとなる。

◎ドームは周辺部の4点からテンション・ロッドにより、8本の空中にのびる円柱の上に支持されて、傾斜した八辺形のドラムをつくり、その上に32面の三角形にトラス組みされたビームが置かれる。このビームにスプリングにのった8個のサポート・ウィールが固定され、その上に先端を切り落した円筒状のドームがのる。

◎ドームは1個のリング・ビームと何個かのパラレル・プレイン・トラスからなる。これらのトラスの中に、横に動くとともに旋回する鏡が吊されて、日光の反射を質と量の2点から、コントロールできるようにする。

This was achieved by placing two rotating domes each 18m in diameter containing robotic mirrors in a new 3D roof of light transmitting, insulated and ventilated double skinned Teflon fabric. The Teflon roof transmits about 2% of the incident light and provides the hierarchical base of light for the space below.

Each dome is supported on 8 flying columns from four perimeter points by tension rods, creating a tapering octagonal drum, upon which is placed a 32 sided triangular trussed beam. To this beam are fixed eight support wheels on springs which carry the truncated cylindrical dome. The dome is composed of a ring beam and parallel plane trusses. Within these trusses are the suspended mirrors which move both laterally and pivot to ensure that the reflected sunlight is controlled in terms of both quantity and quality.

The central roof of the Museum of Science Technology and Industry was conceived to establish a hierarchy of zenithal light entering the Museum, with a clear geometrical of the rectangular area of the entrance hall roof.

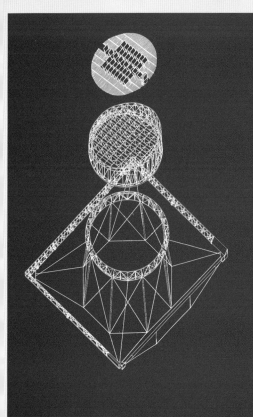

aluminium structure

roof

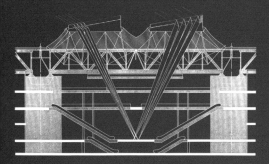

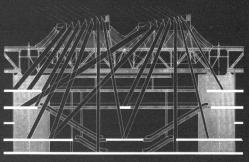

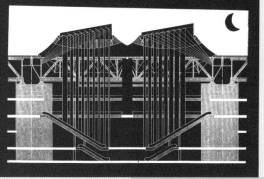

# JAMES STIRLING + MICHAEL WILFORD + PARTNERS LTD.
### ジェームズ・スターリング┼マイケル・ウィルフォード┼パートナーズ・リミテッド

P : Offices＋Shops
T : No.1 Poultry
D : James Stirling＋Michael Wilford＋Partners
C : Peter Palumbo/City Acre Trust
L : London
A : 30,000m²
M : Structural Concrete Frame, Faced with
Sandstone and Granite, with Bronze.

◎この敷地にミース・ヴァン・デル・ローエの設計になるタワーを建てるという先のプランが、ロンドン市都市計画員に拒否されたとき、ピーター・パルンボはこの企画の設計にジェームズ・スターリングを招いた。それは1階と地階にある店、レストランと屋上庭園があるほかに、5階分のオフィスが入る。空に向かって開いた直径36mの円形ドラムの周りに設計されている。そのデザインはチャールズ王子が公共の場で攻撃して、激しい論議の的となった。

Peter Palumbo invited James Stirling to design this scheme when his earlier plan to build a tower designed by Mies van der Rohe for this site was rejected by the city of London planners. It includer five floors of offices, as well as shops on first floor and basement level, a restaurant and roof garde, it is planned around a 36m diameter circular drum, open to the sky. Its design became fiercely controversial when Prince Charles chose to attack it in public.

western view

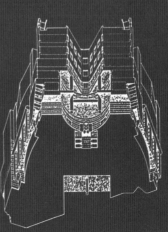

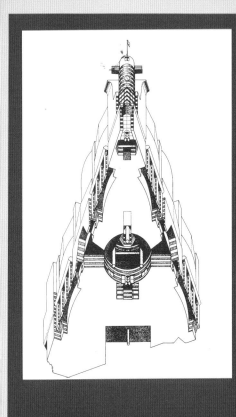

aerial view

from bank

facade

facade

aerial view

P : Science Center
T : Berlin Science Centre
D : James Stirling＋Michael Wilford＋Partners
C : IBA
L : W.Berlin
M : Concrete Structure, Stone and Stucco
    Facades, Steel and Glass Canopies
photo by Richard Bryant

courtyard

revolving door

◎ベルリン市におけるいくつかの新しいプロジェ
クトのひとつとして建設された、このアカデミッ
クな建物は、多数の細胞のようなスペースを含ん
でいる。建築家たちがこの摘要に形をあたえるた
め選んだのは、中世の城の本丸とか、僧院、バシ
リカを含めて、建築の原型ともいうべきものをい
くつか組み込むことだった。その意図は、ひとつ
の連続した建物をつくりだし、それによって、囲
い込まれているという感覚をよび起こす一連のス
ペースで、ガーデン・コートを備えたオックスブ
リッジのカレッジといったひとつ流れのスペース
を創造することにあった。

Constructed as one of a number of new
projects in the city of Berlin, this
academic building contains a large
number of cellular spaces. The architects
have chosen to give form to this brief by
incorporating a number of architectural
archetypes, including a medieval keep, a
cloister, and a basilica. The intention has
been to create a series of linked
buildings that create a series of spaces
that recall the sense of enclosure and
sequential spaces of an Oxbridge
college with its garden courts

canopy

# NICHOLAS GRIMSHAW + PARTNERS LTD.
## ニコラス・グリムショウ＋パートナーズ・リミテッド

P : Printing Works
T : Printing Works For Financial Times
D : Nicholas Grimshaw＋Partners Ltd.
C : Financial Times
L : London
A : 14,000m²
M : Glazed Screens, Steel Frame, Super Plastic
    Aluminium
photo by Joreid＋John Peck

◎建物は縦16m、横96mのガラス壁を通して、2台の大きな構造の複雑な印刷機をA13の通勤客に見せ、建物の内部の機構を明瞭に物語っている。建物のコンテクスト内にこの大きなガラス入りスクリーンをつくりあげるため、非常に緻密なプログラムに、特別な構造上のシステムが開発された。これには実物大プロトタイプの模型づくりとテストが含まれている。
◎開発の目的のひとつには、建物がその機能を果たすだけでなく、ひとつの標識となり、波止場の全般的地域開発のなかで、『ファイナンシャル・タイムズ』の名を確認することができるようにした。

The building is a clear statement of its internal organization with the two large and intricate printing presses visible to commuters on the A13 through a 16m high 96m long glazed wall. To achieve this large glazed screen within the context of the building a special glazing and structural system was developed within the very tight programme. This included modelling and testing of full scale prototypes.
One of the aims of the development is that the building will not only fulfil its function but become a landmark and identify the Financial Times within the overall Docklands development.

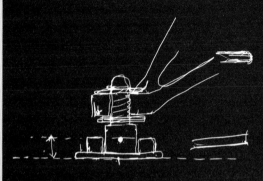

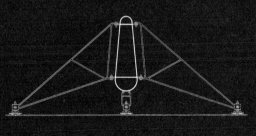

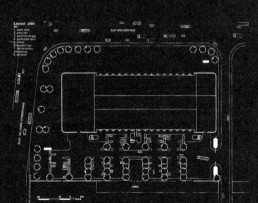

facade

entrance

steel structure

P : Shop
T : Homebase
D : Nicholas Grimshaw＋Partners Ltd
C : Hombase Ltd
L : Brentford, Middlesex
A : 4,250m²
M : Aluminium Sheeting, GRP, Steel, Concrete
photo by Joreid＋John Peck.

◎ この企てのアイディアは、タワーから吊されたスチールのテンション・ロッドにより中間の点に支えられた構造上の背景、これは建物の端から端まであるが、それを使うことによって柱のないスペースをつくりだすことであった。タワーはまた「ホームベース」の看板をのせて、向かい側のジレット・タワーの真似をし、グレート・ウエスト・ロードの劇的な看板の伝統を蘇がえらすことをねらった。四方に開いた高いサービシング・デッキは、地下の駐車場は特に問題なく、ハイ・レベルの駐車場を達成させてくれた。

The idea for the scheme was to create a column-free space by means of a structural spine along the length of the building which was supported at an intermediate point by steel tension rods hung from a tower. The tower was also intended to carry the Homebase sign thus echoing the Gillette tower opposite and reviving the tradition of dramatic signage on the Great West Road. A raised servicing deck open on all sides allowed the high level of car parking to be achieved without the inherent problems of basement car parking.

aluminium roof

car park

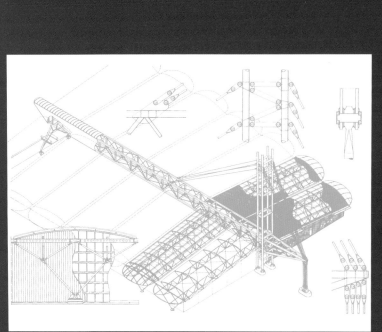

structural tower

rear entrance

P : Ice Rink
T : Oxford Ice Rink
D : Nicholas Grimshaw＋Partners Ltd.
C : City of Oxford
L : Oxford
A : 2,600m²
M : Steel Framework, PVC Membrane, GRC
    Panels, Concrete
photo by Alastain Hunter, Mike Taylor, Three's
Company

◎おもなデザイン上の問題は２つあった。第一は高度に専門化したタイプの建物に、経済的、技術的解決をあたえること、第二は大衆を惹きつける刺激的なイメージを創造することであった。

◎建築上のアプローチはあらゆるアイス・リンク設備を単純なおおいの中に組込み、多くイメージを建物の構造に重ね合せようというものであった。

◎建築上の解決には２つの強力な影響があった。第一は土地の状態であった。それにはくい打ちの必要も含まれた。第二はアイス・パッドに必要なフリー・エリアをとらせてくれる広いスパンが要求されることだった。

◎構造上の問題は屋根の荷重を支える背骨ビームの使用により解決された。荷重は建物のそれぞれの端のマストにかかり、その各々の下にはたった４本のパイル群があるだけである。背骨ビームからの荷重はステンレス・スチールのロッドにより、マストにかかり、マストは建物のエッジ・ビームと、また建物の各々の端の４本のテンション・パイル群にしっかりつなぎ止められて固定された。建物全体にパイルを打ち込む代わりに、わずか16本のパイルが用いられただけである。そして外装材の荷重は周辺部のストリップ基礎にかかるようにした。

◎人と氷の関係については深く考慮された。人々がスムーズにリンクを回れるということを最重要点としてプロジェクトは進められた。さらに開催回数の少ないアイス・ホッケーの試合のために移動式観覧席の設備が用意された。

There were two main design issues. The first was to provide an economic technical solution for a highly specialized type of building. A second was to create an exciting image which would attract the public in large numbers.

The architectural approach was to try to organize all the ice rink facilities under one simple envelope with a lot of image being created by the structure of the building.

There were two powerful influences on the structural solution. The first was the ground conditions, which implied the need for piling, and the second was the need for wide spans to allow the necessary free area for the ice pad.

The structural solution adopted used a spine beam to pick up the majority of the roof load, which was transmitted to a mast at each end of the building, under each of which there was a group of only four piles. The load from the spine beam was transmitted to the mast by stainless steel rods and the masts were stabilized by anchoring them to the edge beam of the building and also to a group of four tension piles at each end of the building. Thus only 16 piles were used instesd of piling the entire building, and the cladding loads were able to rest on simple strip foundations around the perimeter.

The relationship between people and ice was an issue which provoked a lot of thought and discussion. A very important issue was the need for people to circulate freely around the rink. So "pull-out" bleacher seating has been provided for the relatively infrequentice hockey matches.

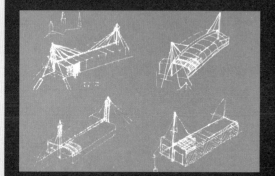

glass wall

structural detail

general view

# PAWSON SILVESTRIN
ポーソン・シルヴェストリン

P : Restaurant
T : Wakaba Japanese Restaurant
D : Pawson Silvestrin
C : Wakaba Japanese Restaurant
L : London
A : 100m$^2$
M : Acid Etched Glass, White Oiled Beech
  Painted Plaster

◎ 正面には酸で食刻したガラスの壁がつくる単一なイメージしかない。この壁はレストランは単調なハムステッドの道路を隔てる神秘的な境界となっている。お客はガラスの壁の美しいカーブに導かれて、入口へと進み、わきに玄関のドアをみいだす。建物の正面には開口部は見えない。中に入ると広々としたスペースが目の前に広がる。ガラスの機能により、視野を外界から断ち、非日常性を演出する。建築材料のすべてを白で統一し、引き壁で仕切り、絵画、植物などのありふれたものを退け、「貧しくみせかけた」床とそれに合わせた家具（白木のブナ材使用）を置いた。劇場風のスクリーンの背後にクロークルームを隠し、すしバーの道具類をラッカー塗りの食器棚にしまうように設計された。

dining area

The facade is nothing but a single image of full tone acid etched translucent glass-wall forming a mysterious edge between the restaurant and the most unsophisticated road in Hampstead. The exquisite curve of the glass-wall leads the customers to the entrance thereby disguising the front door to the side. When viewing the front of the building, the facade-mask has no gaps for breathing or seeing. Once inside the viewer has no distraction other than grasping the mass-space of the open room.
The quality of the glass makes the exterior present yet invisible thus his feeling of relaxed privacy away from the everyday business. The space is rendered by dressing in white paint all the construction materials, zoning the place with freestanding object — dwarf walls, avoiding visual cliches such as pictures, bottles and plants, placing a 'poverty-look' floor and matching furniture (white oiled beech), hiding the cloakroom behind openable theatrical screens and finally concealing the Sushi bar utensils in lacquered cupboards.

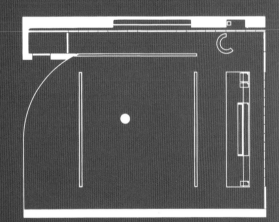

glazed wall

front facade

P : Shop
T : Cannelle Patisserie
D : Pawson Silvestrin
L : London
A : 50m²
M : Painted MDF, Painted Plaster, Acid Etched
    Glass

◎店の通りに面する側は半透明の食刻ガラス壁で、一見しただけでは内部がわからない。マスク・ファサードはニカワで透明ガラスのキューブがはめ込まれて、1個分だけ中を見せるため中央に穴をあけられたような体である。日中は、ガラスがさし込む日光を濾過する。夜には人口照明があやしく光り、魅惑的な効果を生む。透明ガラスのボックスは人を招きよせて、外から中を覗きこませ、外を通る車のライトは、音もなく内部のシーンの一部となる。大理石とステンレス・スチールのカウンターが、小型の壁の後にある。小壁は大またに三段ガラス壁に向かってのぼる。この白い「もの」は準備作業に必要な、無数のこまごましたもの、キャッシュ・マシンからエッスプレッソ・コーヒー・マシンに到るまでを人目から遮っている。

The shop faces the street with a full tone acid etched translucent glazed wall which conceals the interior at the viewer's first sight. The mask-facade is punctured by a clear glass cube, set-in with invisible glue, centrally located for the display of a single cake. During the day, the glass filters the sunlight in; at night, artificial light gives it a mysterious yet fascinating quality. The clear glass box invites people to peer in from the outside and the light of passing traffic gently become part of the interior scene. The marble and stainless steel counter is behind a dwarf wall which steps up toward the glass wall in three bold risers. This white 'object' screens the countless tiny objects needed for preparation work, from the cash machine to the expresso coffee machine.

front facade

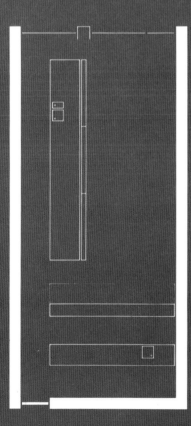

P : Shop
T : Cannelle Patisserie
D : Pawson Silvestrin
L : London
A : 50m²
M : Painted MDF, Painted Plaster, Acid Etched
    Glass

window display

The shop faces the street with a full tone acid etched translucent glazed wall which conceals the interior at the viewer's first sight. The mask-facade is punctured by a clear glass cube, set-in with invisible glue, centrally located for the display of a single cake. During the day, the glass filters the sunlight in; at night, artificial light gives it a mysterious yet fascinating quality. The clear glass box invites people to peer in from the outside and the light of passing traffic gently become part of the interior scene.

P : Exhibition
T : Handtools Exhibition
D : Pawson Silvestrin
C : Conran Foundation
P : Victoria＋Albert Museum
A : 1,200m²
M : Painted MDF, Painted Plaster, Acid Etched
    Glass

◎「分解された」手（プラン参照）に従って置かれた、5分割の壁のオブジェクト。プリズムは見物人が自分自身の習慣的な姿勢を直すため招かれるような方法で手道具を収容している。

A multi directional space made by five cut wall-objects posited according to a 'deconstructed' hand (see plan). The prisms house the handtools in such a way that the viewer's is invited to modify his own body habitual posture.

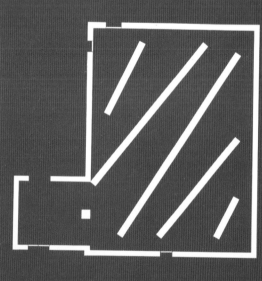

P : Exhibition
T : Handtools Exhibition
D : Pawson Silvestrin
C : Conran Foundation
P : Victoria＋Albert Museum
A : 1,200m²
M : Painted MDF, Painted Plaster, Acid Etched
    Glass

# POWELL-TUCK, CONNOR | OREFELT LTD.
## パウエル　タック, コナー | オルフェルト・リミテッド

P : Design Studio
T : A Studio For A Graphic Designer
D : Powell-Tuck, Connor+Orefelt
C : Michael Hodgeson
L : California
M : Stud Wark, Plywood, Stucco

◎イギリスのグラフィック・デザイナー、マイケル・ホジソンが仕事のためのスタジオを必要としていた。彼は海辺近くに、40年代のトラック・バンガローと裏庭にガレージを所有していた。このガレージに2階を建て増してスタジオに使おうという考えであった。

◎現存する建造物は柱、プラスターと六角目の金網でつくられているにすぎなかった。この地域の規制に従い、ガレージを境界から約60cm離さなければならなかった。上にのせる建造物は最も単純なものになり、柱、プライウッドとスタッフの箱が、ガレージと角度を保ち置かれ、階段が設置された。

◎南の窓はカリフォルニアの太陽を遮ぎるため小さくしてある。スタジオの大きな窓は西北向きだが、それでも十分な明かりを取り入れることができる。窓はすべて規格品で、大きな窓は4種の異なるサイズからなり、ともに取りつけてある。

◎スタジオは、高くて、非常に変わったスタイル……これは新しいベニス四角形である……なので、この地に降りたった宇宙船のように見える。

◎このプロジェクトで最も成功したことは、コストが全体で4万ドルしかかからなかったことである。

Michael Hodgeson, a British Graphic Designer, needed a studio to carry out his works. He owned a 40's track bungalow near the beach, with an exiting garage in the backgarden. The idea was to add a second floor to the garage for use as a studio.

The existing structure which was only constructed front stud, plaster and chicken wire, however because of local regulations we had to move the garage two feet away from the boundary. The construction on top is of the most simple type it is a box of stud, plywood and stucco, set at an angle to the existing garage and a staircase added.

The windows to the South are small to keep out the Californian sun. The large studio window faces North West and can still let in good quality light. All of the windows are standard and the large window consists of 4 diffelent sizes, fixed together.

The studio sits like an alien craft in this area being higher very different in style — this is the new Venice rectangular.

The most successful aspect of this project was the cost of the whole construction cost $40,000.

work space

fifties' freezer

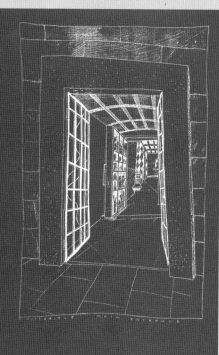

P : Restaurant, Club
T : Vittoriale—House of Pleasure
D : Powll-Tuck, Connor＋Orefelt
L : Tokyo
AD : Hiroshi Shioi

◎ 建物全体にわたって、イメージが歪められ、超現実的であり、時の流れを感じさせない。建物はまさに今、現在であり、歴史的スタイルを模倣したものではない。ユニークで、快適であるとともに風変わりでもある……お客が食事をし、談話するところは、心地よく、美しく、楽しませてくれるスペースである。玄関、ホール、階段、謁見の間、塔などは風変わりで、通り過ぎて眺めるだけでも心をはずませる。建物と家具は歪められ、ろうそくの照明、色ガラス、音響が独自の雰囲気をかもし出すために使われている……。
◎ エレベーターは、地階にある2つのキッチンから上のレストランへ料理を運ぶのに使用されるだけで、人の乗れるエレベーターは1台もない──ここを訪れる人すべてに建物を体で知ってもらうためである。

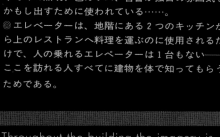

Throughout the building the imagery is distorted, surreal but never historic. The building is modern, of today, and will never be a pastishe of some historic style. It will be unique, both comfortable and strange......comfortable, beautiful, flattering where guest's dine and converse; strange and exhilarating in spaces to pass through and view, the entrance, hall, the stair, the inner stair, the throne room and tower. Architecture and furniture is distorted, lighting by candles, tinted glass, sounds are used to create an atmosphere......
The highest technology available can be used to convey food from the two basement floor kitchens to the restaurants above, and yet there is not passenger lift — the building demands to be experienced by all who visit it.

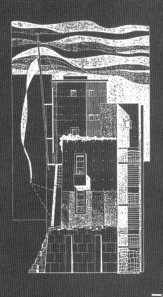

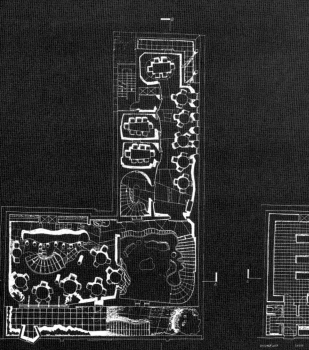

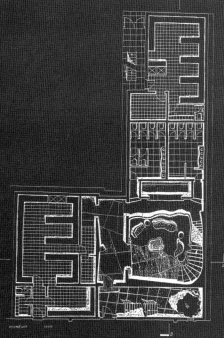

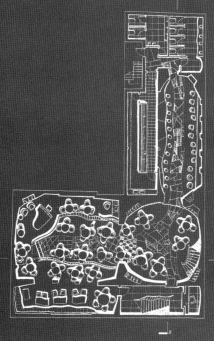

P : House
T : Villa Zapu
D : Powell-Tuck, Connor＋Orefelt
C : Private Client
L : California
A : 850m²
M : Stucco Render on Timber Frame and
    Plywood
photo by Richard Waite

◎家のための敷地は北から南へ走る高い屋根の最高部である。新しい建物は屋根を横切る何段かのバリアを形づくっている。

◎家の南側が入口になっており、第一のバリアは白い壁が立ちふさがり、小さなドアがある。訪問客は車から降りて、芝生の空地を徒歩で横切ってメイン・ファサードへと近づく。

◎主屋のプランは細くて長く、東西の軸にのる。これは南側から最大限に日光を入れ、北側の眺望を楽しむためである。リビングルームやマスター・ベッドルームは南北両方の面をもつ。

◎客用の独立家屋にある北側のタワーは、以前は1階の北側が入口だった。中のスペースは3倍の高さをもつ居間で、バック・スクリーンは開くが眺望はほとんどきかず、窓も少ない。1階はキッチンとダイニング・ルームである。タワーにはまたバス、子供用ベッドルームもあり、最上階に眺めのすばらしいマスター・ベッドルームがあり、すべてが「中世風」らせん階段で結ばれている。

The site chosen for the house is on top of a prominent ridge running from north to south. The new building forms a series of barriers across the ridge.

As the house is approached from the south the first barrier is a white wall blocking the road, with a small door. The visitor has to leave his car and approach the main facade across a lawned glade on foot.

The plan of the main house is long thin and on the east west axis, this is in order to give maximum sunlight from the south and views to the north, important spaces as the Living Room and Master Bedroom can therefore have both aspects.

The tower to the north in an independent house for guests, is entered formerly from the north on the first floor. The space entered is a triple height sitting room, the back screen opens with little look outs and windows. The first floor is the kitchen/dining room. The tower also has bathroom, childs bedroom and at the top the master bedroom with wonderful views out, all connected by a 'medieval' spiral stair case.

villa from pool

guest tower

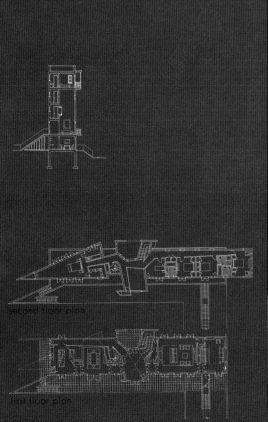

second floor plan

first floor plan

window bay

villa at sunset

interior

from Napa Valley

# RICHARD ROGERS+PARTNERS
## リチャード・ロジャース+パートナーズ

P : Office
T : Old Billingsgate Market
D : Richard Rogers+Partners
C : Citicorp/Citibank
L : London
A : 11,200m²
photo by Richard Bryante

◎元からある2倍の高さの煉瓦製アーチづくり天井をもつ最下部は修復され、中2階レベルが、オープン・プラン・オフィスとして利用するためつくりだされた。中央の各間は2倍の高さのスペースとして残され、サラダ・バーに変えられた。
◎外部の北と南のアーチの埋め込みは、石のアーチのアーケードから引込んだ構造上のグレージングにより達成された。
◎元からある身長大で、むき出しのガラスの屋根窓は「プリズム・ガラス」に入れ替えた。これはアクリル樹脂のプリズムでできていて、間に挟まれて二重ガラス入りユニットにされたひとつの面で反射される。この面の角度は日光が建物にさし込む角度によって決まる。このシステムは自然光を取り入れ、商業用のフロアのVDUスクリーンの拡散にギラギラした光りや反射を生じさす直接光線を反射する。——メイン・ホールにはHプランの中2階レベルを導入して、余分なフロア・レベルが生みだされた。
◎管状のトラス構造がフロアの奥行と容積を最小にするために設計されている。それは中央道路に沿う既存のスチール・ジャック・アーチから宙吊りにされ、北と南の翼の管状スチール柱に支えられている。

mezzanine

The original double height brick vaulted basement has been restored and a mezzanine level created for open plan office use. The central bays have been retained as a double height space and converted into a salad bar.
The infill of the external North and South arches is achieved by structural glazing set back from the stone arched arcade. The full height original open glass louvres are replaced by 'prism glass'. This comprises an acrylic prism, mirrored on one facet sandwiched in double glazed units. The angle of the facets is determined by the angle at which sun penetrates the building. This system allows natural light in but reflects out direct sunlight which could cause glare and reflections on the proliferation of VDU screens on the trading floor.
Additional floor area has been created in the main halls by the introduction of an H Plan mezzanine level.
The tubular truss structure is designed to minimize the depth and bulk of the floor. It is suspended from the existing steel jack arches along the central aisle and supported on tubular steel columns in the North and South wings.

basement floor plan

Billingsgate market

main hall

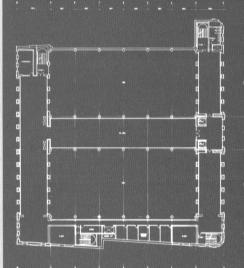

second floor plan

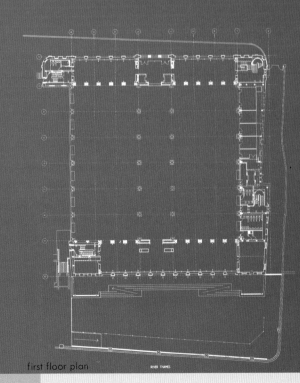

first floor plan    RIVER THAMES

interior

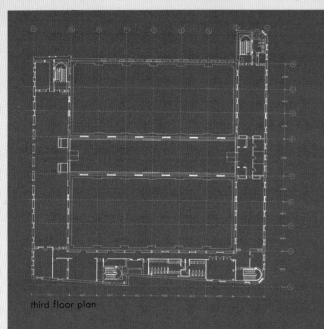
third floor plan

elevation

elevation

P : Factory
T : Inmos Microprocessor Factory
D : Richard Rogers＋Partners
C : Inmos Limited
L : South Wales
A : 8,900m²
M : Tubular Steel Assisted Span Tension Structure

◎速かに建てられるパーツのキットとして、1階建スチール構造として開発された建物デザイン。一区画ごとに建てられるよう、最大限に工場でプレファブリケーションされる。

◎建物のフェイズ1というコンセプトは中央の直線的サーキュレーション、および専門化した活動のため内部翼をそなえたサービス・スパインである。幅7.2m、長さ106mのスパインは内部の通路または情報のプロムナードとして働き、自動販売機、公共電話、座席設備、会議室、オフィスのための植物のある地域と待合室などを収容するのに十分なほどの広さをもつ。そこは目に見えるトータル的な安全管理が用意されており、その敷地にある建物が将来もつ他の面と関連するよう目論まれていて、そのために建物のあらゆる設備は、全スタッフが容易に利用できる。

The building design evolved as a single-storey steel structure conceived as a kit of rapidly erectable parts, with maximum off-site prefabrication to allow the building to be erected day by day. The basic concept of Phase 1 of the building is a central linear circulation and service spine with internal wings for specialized actaivities. The spine 7.2m wide and 106m long, acts as an internal street or informal promenade, generous enough in size to contain vending machines, public telephones, seating, meeting places, planted areas and waiting areas for the offices. It provides total visual security control and is intended to link up with other future phases of building on the site, so that all the facilities in all the buildings are readily available to all staff.

west elevation

west entrance

original sketch

entrance towers

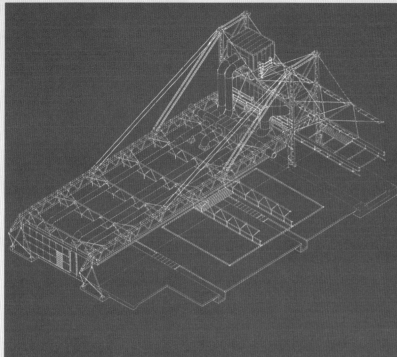

central column

central column

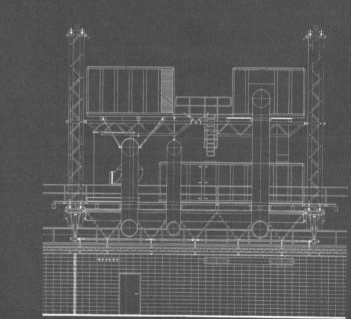

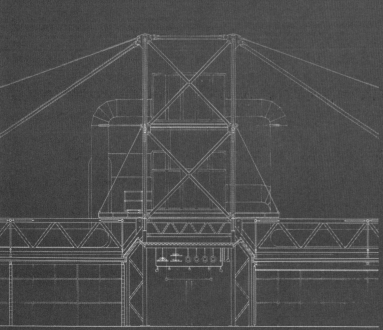

ventilation

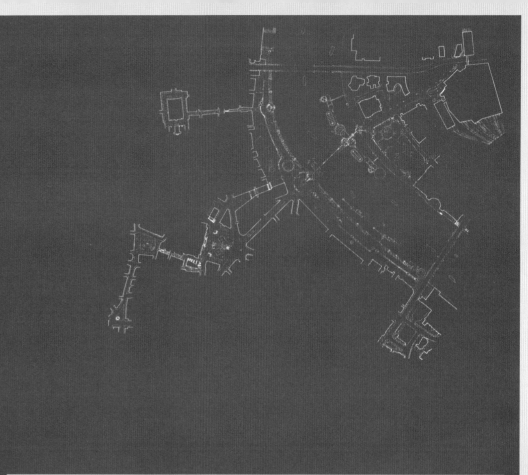

◎ロイヤル・アカデミーでの展示会に招かれて、以前の都市プロジェクトで発表されたアイディアが実践に移され、ロンドンに変身したロンドンの未来像を提示した。介入する領域は2本の軸に沿っていた。第一はトラファルガー広場からウォーターロー駅へ向かう軸、第二はウェストミンスターとブラックファイアーズ橋の間のエンバンクメント沿いと、雑踏するエンバンクメント通りを迂回してリバー・トンネルに入る軸である。プロジェクトの目標は歩行者領域がこれ以上衰退するのをとどめ、川を蘇がえらせ、サウス・バンクの孤立を防ぐことにあった。

◎現在、ハンガーフォード鉄橋がテムズ川の大蛇行部の眺めと、北バンクの一番美しい所の眺めを遮っている。その高架橋が北側のエンバンクメント庭園を二分し、ノーサンバーランド通りを切り離しており、南側のバンクではウォーターロー駅からの眺めをぶち壊し、アート・コンプレックスを分断している。提案によると、6本ある鉄橋を細い歩行者用の吊橋に替え、チャーリング・クロス鉄道交通をウォーターロー東駅で終点にする予定である。

The invitatipn to exhibit at the Royal Academy gave the Practice the opportunity to consolidate ideas and aims identified in previous urban projects, and present London with a vision of a London transformed. The area of intervention stretched along two axis; The first Trafalgar Square to Waterloo Station; the second along the embankments between Westminster and Blackfriars' Bridge, and the diversion of the busy Embankment Road into a river tunnel. The aim of the project was to halt the further decline of the pedestrian's realm, and to revitalize the river and break the isolation of the South Bank At present Hungerford Railway Bridge blocks off views of the great bend in the river and of the north bank at its most handsome. Its viaduct bisects the north side embankment gardens and cuts off Northumberland Avenue, and on the South Bank wrecks views from and of Waterloo Station and disrupts the Arts Complex. The proposal is to replace the six track railway bridge with a slim suspended footbridge with Charing Cross rail traffic terminated at Waterloo East Station.

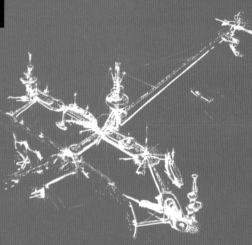

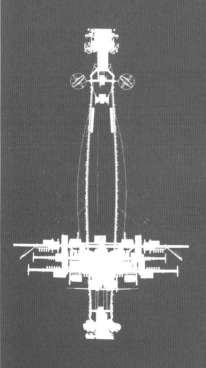

P : Hotel
T : Kabuki-cho
D : Richard Rogers + Partners
C : K1 Corporation
L : Tokyo
A : 2,000m²

◎ このビジネスホテルは、東京の中心にある色彩豊かな地域の小さな通りに面する。ライト・コーンの要求から、建物の大部分は敷地の後部に寄せられ、こうして直接道路に面する地域を一段低くつくった庭として使えることになった。この庭にはスチールの橋がかかり、1階のエントランス・ロビーと受付に通じるアクセスとなっている。建物自体は中央のアクセス・ゾーンにより結ばれたスチールの、マストのような構造に差し込まれた設備ユニットからなっている。露出したリフトと階段が建物の正面にあり、これもその垂直性を強調している。

This business-type hotel faces a small street in the heart of one of Tokyo's more colourful areas. Light cone requirements dictated that the bulk of the building be located to the rear of the site thus liberating the area immediately adjacent to the road as a sunken garden. A steel bridge spans this garden and gives access to the first floor entrance lobby and reception areas. The building itself is comprized of accommodation units plugged into a steel, mast-like structure linked by a central access zone. Exposed lifts and staircases are located to the front of the building and also serve to reinforce its verticality.

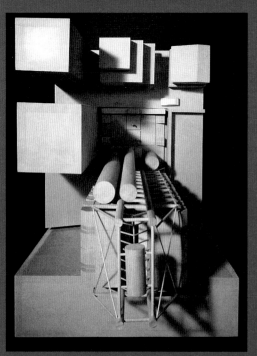

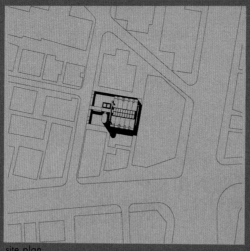

site plan

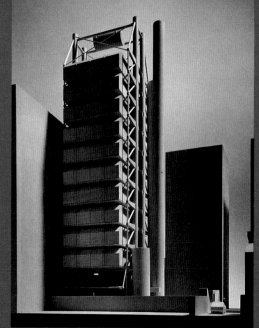

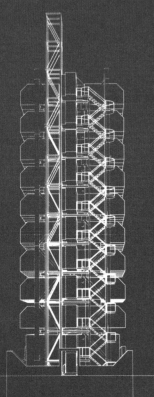

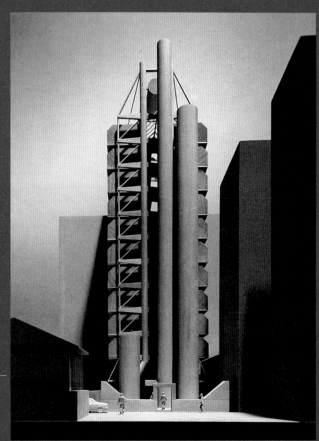

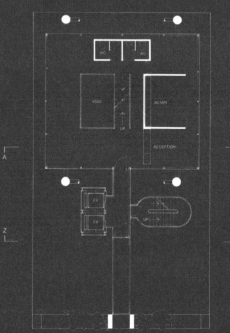

first floor plan

◎飯倉の敷地は東京の中央部にある東京タワーと、ロシア大使館に近い、交通の激しい主要道路に面する。企画の発展に影響をあたえた要因には、隣のノア・ビルがある。これは数年前に白井静一氏が設計したモノリティック仕上げの黒い建物である。その他に立地が飯倉交差点のすぐ南にある急な傾斜地ということがある。
◎各階が上から下までのガラス入りで、露出した構造とサーチライト・タワーと相まって宝石のような外観に透明性を生みだしている。建物自体は地下の駐車システム、地下レストラン、１階のショールームとその上に８階分あるオフィス施設からなる。オフィス・スペースに構造上、または核となるエレメントがないため、広々とした、フレキシブルな環境をつくりだしている。

P : Office
T : Iikura
D : Richard Rogers＋Partners
C : K1 Corporation
L : Tokyo
A : 2,700m²
photo by Masaaki Sekiya

The Iikura site faces a busy main road near to the Tokyo Tower and to the Russian Embassy in central Tokyo. Among the factors which have influenced the development of the scheme are the adjacent NOA building, a monolithic black structure designed some years ago by Shirai Seiichi and its location on a steep incline just sorth of the Iikura crossing.
Full height glazing on each floor, together with the exposed structure and satellite tower produces a transparency which invokes a fine, jewel-like appearance. The building itself is comprized of a basement parking system, basement restaurant, a first floor showroom and 8 floors of office accommodation above. The absence of structural or core elements in the office space creates an open and flexible environment.

east facade

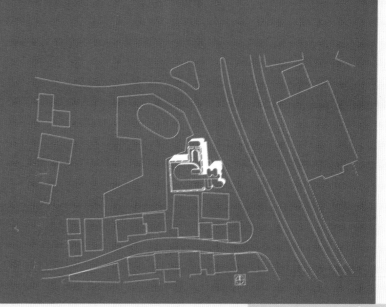

# RON ARAD/ONE OFF
ロン・アラッド／ワン・オフ

P : Design Studio, Shop
T : One Off
D : Ron Arad
C : One Off
L : London
A : 185m$^2$
M : Steel

doorway

shop

shop

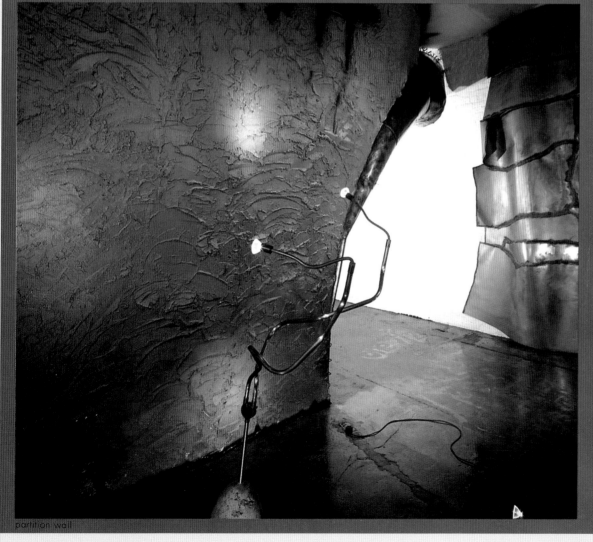

partition wall

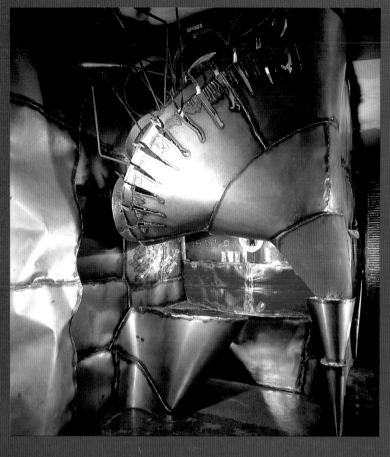

completed detail

a customer

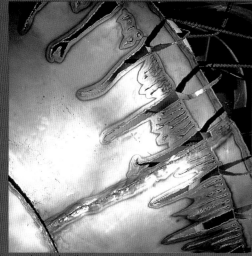

completed detail

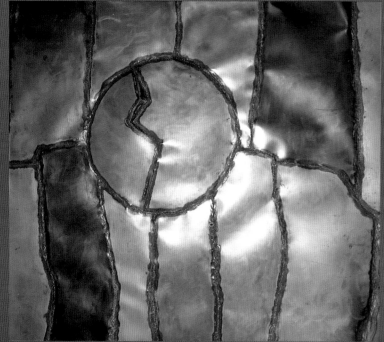

completed detail

completed detail

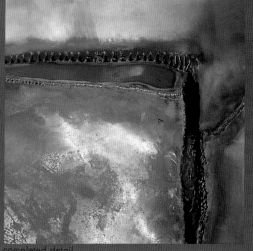

completed detail

P : Design Studio
T : The Bureaux
D : Ron Arad
L : London
A : 460m²
M : Timber, Steel, Glass

general view

table

lamp

meeting room

staircase

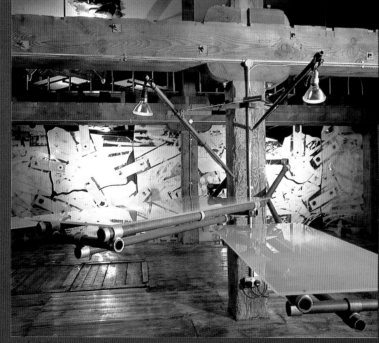

work-station

meeting area

P : Shop
T : Gaultier For Women
D : Ron Arad
C : Jean Paul-Gaultier
L : London
A : 45m²
M : Concrete, Steel

interior

mannequin

# SIMON CONDER ASSOCIATES
サイモン・コンダー・アソシエーツ

P : Apartment
T : Laval Penthouse
D : Simon Conder Associates
C : Mr & Mrs Laval
L : London
A : 250m$^2$
M : Studwork, Plasterboard, Marble, Ash and
    Brass Strips. Painted Plaster, Joinery
    Cellulose Sprayed in Situ

◎このプランを限定する要素は湾曲した背骨状の壁で、それにより訪問客はアパートのエントランスから主要な居住部分と、一段高い温室へと導かれる。
◎この壁の設計には円形の階段エンクロージャーと慎重に結合されて、すばらしい眺望を訪問客に垣間見せてくれる。特に、エントランス・ホールから見えるリバーサイドのガラス壁の区域は、テムズ川の対岸にあるホークスムアー教会の塔を1枚の絵のように見せるよう、慎重に決められた。
◎大理石のフローリングはその上の円いマッキントッシュ・テーブルと、そのテーブルの脚をのせるために用いられた、磨いたトネリコ材と真ちゅうのインサートによくうつるよう、注意深く配置された。温室へ通じる、新しくつくられた段のけあげは、段そのものに用いられた黒いマルキナ・マーブルとコントラストをなすよう白いペンタリコン・マーブルから選ばれ、それによってリビングとダイニングの間の、レベルの変化を強調している。
◎フラットのデザインにはそれ自体の構造で立つ家具が選択された。黒いマッキントッシュのテーブルとイングラムの椅子はやや様式的なリバーサイドの正面をもつ、ガラス仕様ダイニング・エリアにとりわけ適していると考えられ、エイリーン・グレイとル・コルビジェによるモダン・クラシックスは、フラットの白いエリアと類似性をもたせるために選ばれた。

living room

The key defining element in the plan is a curved spine wall which leads the visitor through from the flat entrance to the main living area and the raised conservatory. The setting out of this wall has been carefully combined with the circular staircase enclosure to give the visitor just a glimpse of the exciting views to come. In particular the small area of the riverside glazed wall which can be seen from the entrance hall has been carefully defined to frame the tower of the Hawksmoor chrch on the other side of the Thames.

The marble flooring has been carefully laid out to reflect the circular Mackintosh table above with inserts of polished ash and brass used to locate the legs of the table. The risers of the newly formed steps to the conservatory area have been picked out in a white Pentalicon marble to contrast with the black Marquina marble used on the steps themselves and thereby reinforce the differentiation between the living and dinig areas that the change in level implies.

The desigh of the flat included the choice of the free standing furniture. The black Mackintosh table and Ingram chairs were thought particularly appropriate to the glazed dining area with its rather mannered riverside elevation and modern classics by Eileen Gray and Le Corbusier were similarly chosen for their obvious affinities with the white areas of the flat.

corridor

kitchen

P : Apartment
T : Butlers Wharf Upstream Penthouse
D : Simon Conder Associates
C : Dual Developments Limited
L : London
A : 375m²
M : Oak, Granite, Marble, Venetian Plaster,
    Nickel Plated, Iron Mongery Armour Plate
    Glass, Acid Etched Glass, Steel

◎ デザインのおもな目標は２つのフロアを同じ線で貫き、その重要性（この場合ベージュのベネチアン・プラスター仕上げが用いられた）を示すため特別な仕上げで設計され、中央の背骨壁をつくることであった。必要な所でこの壁を分断し、貫く形で、フラットのプランはこの壁の周りに、積極的に展開された。ダイニングとラウンジのエリアの限界として、たとえばファイアプレースを入れたり、開口部の枠としている。他方で同時に２つのフロアの間に具体的な絆を提供し、ペントハウスを統一している。おもな階段とランディングの交差、フラットの中央の壁が、企画の劇的なセンターピースとなる一方で、低まったハーフ・ランディングが訪問客を、近くにあるタワー・ブリッジの一番すばらしい眺めに向かせてくれる。

The main objectives of the disigh were to create a central spine wall to the flat that ran through both floors on the same line and was picked out in a 'particular' finish to indicate its importance (in this instance a beige Venetian plaster finish was used). By fragmenting and piercing this wall where required the plan of the flat worked around this wall in a positive way; suggesting the limits of the dining and lounge areas, housing a fireplace or framing an opening for example, while at the same time providing a strong tangible bond between the two floors, unifying the penthose. The intersection of the main staircase and landing, and the wall in the centre of the flat provides a dramatic centrepiece to the scheme while the lowered half landing orientates the visitor for the best view of nearby Tower Bridge.

central area

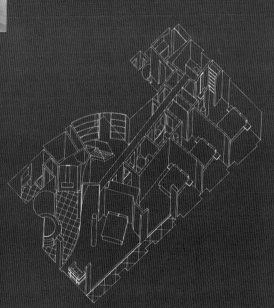

steps

landing

P : Workshop
T : Stradbroke Rurar Workshop
D : Simon Condor Associates with Jon Broome
C : English Estates
L : Suffolk
A : 1,500m$^2$
M : Steel Framework, PVC, Coated Corrugated
    Steel, Woodwool, Blockwork

◎ 総体的企画の主要コンセプトは人間的な尺度と、サフォークの地方的伝統とを結びつけ、強い地縁をもつなかで働くためのコミュニティを創造することであった。
◎ レイアウトと形は伝統的な農家の家屋からとり、急勾配の屋根が、コートヤードを囲い込む建物が基盤となっている。周辺のレイアウトも高密度の開発を可能にした。
◎ 企画の方向性が内部に向かっているにもかかわらず、建物の間から、そして小さな窓を通して、各ワークショップから、周りの風景を眺めることができる。
◎ 外装材の形と色は、風にさらされる風景のなかで保護的な性質をそなえ、この地方で伝統的に用いられる黒塗りの下見板と茅ぶきや瓦ぶき屋根の代用とされた黒い波板と結びつけて選ばれた。

The primary objective of the overall scheme was to create a working community with a human scale and a strong sense of place related to local Suffolk traditions.
The layout and forms derive from traditional farm buildings and are based on buildings with steep pitched roofs enclosing a sheltered courtyard space which forms the focus of the scheme. The perimeter layout also enables a relatively high density of development.
Although the character of the scheme is essentially inward looking, there are views out into the surrounding landscape through the gaps between the buildings and from within each workshop through small windows.
The form and colour of the materials on the exterior of the scheme have been chosen to provide a protective quality in a windswept landscape and relate to the traditional lacal use of black-stained weatherboarding and the frequent replacement of thatched and tiled roofs with black corrugated sheeting.

interior

workshops

building gables

P : Harbour Entrance
T : Sealink Port Areas
D : Simon Condor Associates
C : Sealink Plc.
L : Folkestone Kent
A : 12m$^2$
M : Powder Coated Mild Steel, Tubular Steel,
    Masonry Walling

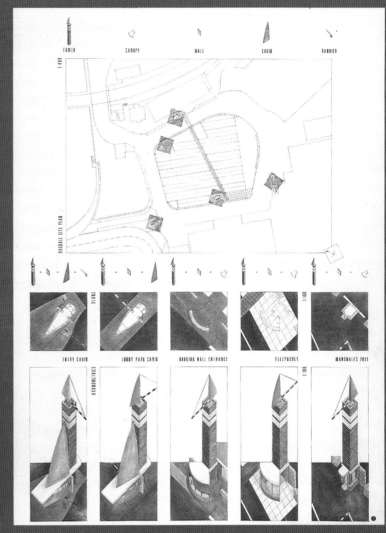

◎パーツの基本的キットはタワー１基、石造りの壁の部分いくつかと、一続きの片持ち梁の天蓋からなる。
◎タワーは計画で高さ12m、1.5m²の円筒形のスチールの構造物でできている。
◎これにはシーリンクの会社のカラーであるブルーと黄色で、パウダーをコートしたポリエステルの保護仕上げした軟鋼の小割板がかぶせてある。高い部分の黄色い板には一面に穴が開けられていて、タワー内部の強力な照明がこの穴からもれ周囲を照らす。低い所ではこれらの小板は、シーリングの現在のグラフィック・アイデンティティーを用いて、明確な標識システムの基本として使われる。
◎タワーの頂上には高さ3.5mの強力な風向計があり、マリン・プライと薄いゲージのステンレス・スチール板でおおわれたスチールのフレームとしてつくられている。風向計は風に従って位置を変え、海からフォークストーンに近づく人たちにはドラマチックな陸地の姿を見ることができる。

The primary kit of parts consists of a tower, some short sections of masonry walling and a series of cantilevered canopies.
The tower consists of a tubular framed steel structure 12m high and 1.5m square on plan.
This is clad in mild steel slats with a power coated polyester protective finish in the Sealink Blue and Yellow corporate colours. The yellow slats at high level are densely perforated to allow the high intensity lighting contained in this section of the tower to flood the surrounding area. At lower levels these slats would be used as the basis of a comprehensive signing system using Sealink's existing graphic identity.
At the top of the tower there is a 3.5m high wind vane constructed as a steel frame clad in marine ply and thin guage stainless steel sheeting. The wind vanes will abjust their position according to the prevailing wind and present a dramatic landfall to those approaching Folkestone from the sea.

# STANTON WILLIAMS
スタントン・ウィリアムズ

P : Shop
T : Issey Miyake Men's Shop
D : Stanton Williams
C : Issey Miyake
L : London
A : 66m²
M : Marmorina Plaster, Stone, Glass English Oak

◎狭い4階建の店舗ビルを示されて、われわれは三宅氏の繊細なファブリックと強烈なフォームに、単純な素材を用いたドラマチックな空間をつくることによって応えた。元の建物の床ははがされ、壁と天井はマルモリアン・プラスターを使用した。幅広の石の階段がエントランスから下へ降りて衣服が展示されているアルコーブへと通じる。エントランス・ドアと家具はイングリッシュ・オーク材を使っている。
◎店の後側では、ルーフライトが大量の日光を垂直に取り入れる。他の照明は天井や壁のしぼみに隠されている。

Given the context (a narrow four storey shop building) responded to Miyake's subtle fabrics and strong forms by building a dramatic space with rich but simple materials. Two floors were removed from the original building and walls and celings rendered in Italian Marmorina plaster. A wide stone stair moves downwards from the entrance to the alcoves where the clothes are displayed. Entrance doors and furniture are in English oak.
At the rear of the shop, a rooflight brings daylight vertically down through the volume. Other (artificial) lighting is hidden or recessed in ceiling or wall cavities.

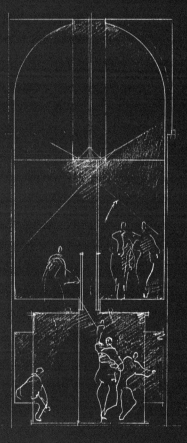

first floor

entrance

# TREVOR HORNE ARCHITECTS
## トレヴァ・ホーン・アーキテクツ

P : House
T : Flask Walk
D : Trevor Horne Architects
C : Richard and Mark Shipman
L : London
A : 120m²
M : Plaster, MDF, Neon, Ash, Oak, Stainless
    Steel
photo by Ed Ironside

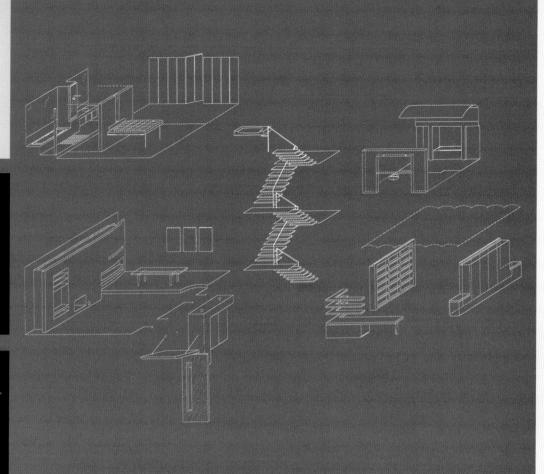

◎ レベルを異にする2つの独立した部屋が、時には床にふれ、時には両方のスペースを浮遊する、湾曲したスクリーンで結び合わされる。ネオン灯、弱いタングステン灯がバックライトやスポットライトとして新しいエレメントを照しだす。
◎ このスクリーンの家は火、回転したりスライドしたりするTVトレー、CD、サウンド・システム・レコード、カセット保管ケースおよび飲食をおおっている。

Two disjointed rooms with a level
difference are tied together by a curving
screen that sometimes touches the ground,
sometimes floats across both spaces.
Neon, low intensity and tungsten lights
backlight, wash, spotlight and play on
this new element.
The screen houses a fire, a swivelling
sliding TV tray, C. D. , sound systems,
records and cassette storage and drinks.

lounge

handrail

lounge

# TROUGHTON MCASLAN LTD.
## トゥロートン・マッカスラン・リミテッド

P : Studio, Work Space
T : 3 ST. Peters Streel
D : Troughton Mcaslan
C : Derwent Valley Holdings Plc./Colebrook Estates
L : London
A : 420m²
M : Painted Plaster/Brickwood, Steel, Glass Blocks, Timber Flooring

◎広大な6,000平方フィートのワークショップ・ビルディングをビーエルが使うに適した、スタジオとワークスペースに改造する。メイン・セクションは2倍の高さの受付エリアと、約4,000平方フィートの2つの床にまたがる開いた部分と、約1,500平方フィートの連絡廊下でメイン・スペースとつながる、2階建ての前面の建物からなる。
◎テザインは既存の配置の複雑さと不規則性を解決し、ビーエルのユーザーに適した結合力ある開発の創造を試みている。

Conversion of redundant 6,000sf Workshop building into studio and work space suitable for Bl use. Main section consisting of double height reception area and open volumes on two floors of aproximately 4,000sf, and a two floored front building connected to the main spaces by linking corridors of approximately 1,500sf.
Desigh attempts to resolve comlexities and irregularities in the existing arrangement, and to create a cohesive development suitable for a range of Bl users.

studio interior

studio exterior

entrance at night

entrance

P : Offices
T : Shepherd's Bush offices
D : Troughton Mcaslan
C : Michael Peter's Group
L : London
A : 3,000m²

◎マイクル・ピーターのグループのために、建物の内部を除去して、スタジオとオフィスとなる3つの床をもつ内部スペースをつくった。インテリアだけでなく家具と照明もデザインした。
◎ユーティリティ・ルームは両端に隠され、建物の乱雑さを吸収し、大きな中央スペースを比較的きれいに残した。このデザイン・グループが現在上の2つのフロアしか使っていないので、受付ボックスは2階に置かれている。しかし将来の拡張や配置替えを見込んで、完全に解体できるようにしてある。同様に3階の床のスラブにあるような長いスロットが2階の床からも切られて、取り替えられた。必要なとき、アトリウムが3階分の高さにまで延長できるようにするためである。

We gutted the inside of the building to form the new three floor interior space which acts as studios and offices for the Michael Peter's Group.
We designed the furniture and lighting as well as the interiors.
Service and utility rooms are neatly tucked away at eight end, absorbing the irregularities of the building and leaving the large central space relatively clear. Because the desigh group currently occupies only the top two floors the reception box is at first floor level, but it is completely demountable to allow for future expansion/relocation. Similarly, along slot like that in the third floor slab has also been cut out of the second floor, and replaced, so that the atrium can be extended to a full triple-storey height if and when it is required.

reception

first floor

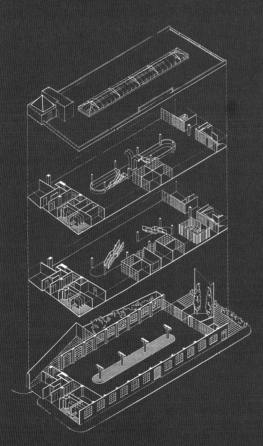

atrium

P : Office
T : Apple Computers Facility
D : Troughton Mcaslan
C : Apple Computers Plc./Stockley Park
    Consortium
L : London
A : 4,600m²

◎ デザインの目標は建物の利用法を反映したプランとセクションに、明確なダイヤグラムをつくりだし、建物内のそれらエレメントを活性化することにあった。中央アーケード、エントランス、開かれた、ダイナミックな仕事の環境を求めるアップルの必要に関連する、開いた空間とサーキュレーションなどである。用いられた素材は、カルウォール半透明外壁材、公共エリアの木材の床、高度な内部植栽、白い清潔な表面などはクライアントの「開放的な」性質とアメリカ西海岸にルーツをもつことに応えたものである。

The aim of the disigh was to produce a clear diagram on plan and section which reflected the building's use, and to energize those elements in the building — central arcade, entrances, open volumes and cirulation which would relate to Apple's need for an open and dynamic working environment. The materials we chose to use — Kalwall translucent external walling, timber floors in public areas, high degree of internal planting, white clean surfaces etc, were in response to the 'open' nature of the client and their US West Coast roots.

exterior

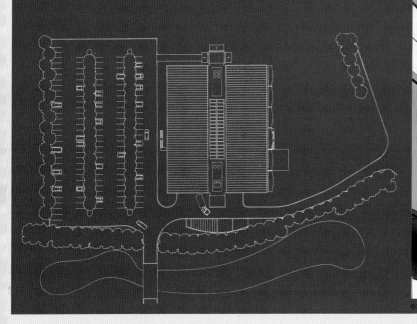

exterior

staircase

second floor plan

office

lobby

first floor plan

# WICKHAM+ASSOCIATES ARCHITECTS
ウィッカム+アソシエーツ・アーキテクツ

P : Housing Offices and Shops
T : Horselydown Square
D : Wickham+Associates
C : Berkey House Docklands Development Ltd.
L : London
A : 14,000m²
M : Brick, Terracotta, Render, Steel
photo by Peter Cook

◎プロジェクトは下の階に店舗やオフィス、上に
アパートのある都市における密度の濃い生活をつ
くり直すことにあった。アパートメントはル・コ
ルビジェによるマルセーユ・ブロックの「リユ・
アンテリエール」と同じような内部のコリドール
・アクセスの辺りに配置される。上部のアパート
メントは近隣の街路を見下ろす大きなテラスに面
している。端のアパートは3階で小塔部屋が屋根
から突き出ている。これらの小塔は、建物の円形
の端によってつくりだされた旋回運動が行きつく
最高点であり、タワー・ブリッジ、テムズ川そし
て街のほうに湾曲するメイン・スクエアへの入口
の目印となる。
◎建物は細部が豊かで、色彩が躍動している。張
りだし窓が煉瓦の壁から突き出ており、バルコニ
ーは建物本体に彫り込まれて、大規模に見せ、テ
ラコッタ・レンダーの大きなパネルがタワー・ブ
リッジ近くのエントランスにまとめてつけてある。
◎デザイン全体が都会的な建築と街の建物の再生
したことを示す、不均一な作品である。

aerial view

The project aims to recreate the density
and life of the city with shops and offices
on the lower floors and apartments
above. The apartments are arranged
about an internal corridor access similar
to the 'rue interior' of the Marseille block
by Le Corbusier. The upper apartments
give onto large terraces overlooking the
neighbouring streets. The end apartments
are three stories high with Turret rooms
emerging through the roof. These turrets
are the culmination of a spiraling
movement set up by the circular ends of
the buildings and mark the entrance to
the Main Square which inflects back to
Tower Bridge, the river and the City.
The buildings are rich in detail and
vibrate with colour. Oriel windows
project from the brick walls, balconies
are carved into the body of the building
creating a giant scale and large panels
of terracotta render press together at the
entrances near Tower Bridge.
The whole disigh is a heterogeneous
composition providing evidence of a
commitment to the revival of an urban
architecture and the art of city building.

terraces

detail

second floor plan

western view

west face

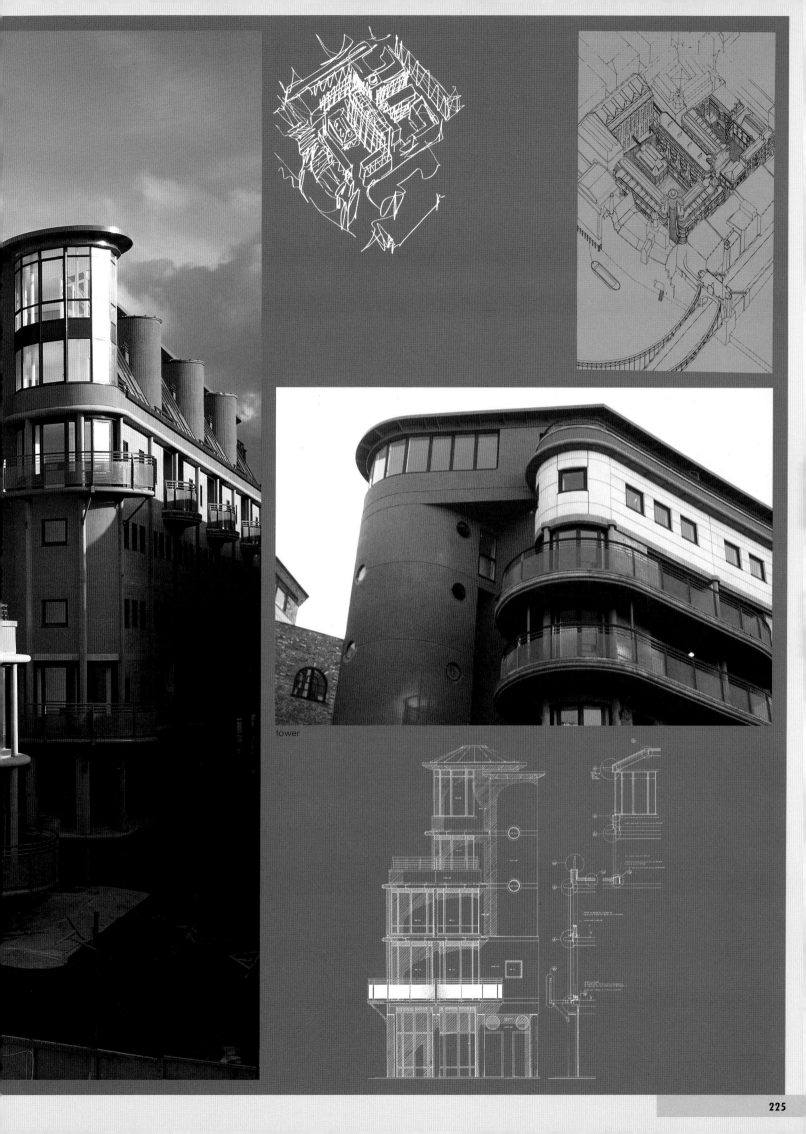

tower

P : Restaurant, Bar
T : Kensington Place Restaurant
D : Wickham＋Associates
C : Simon Slater and Christopher Smallwood
L : London
A : 260m²
M : Steel, Glass, Aluminuim, Rubber, MDF,
　　Cherry, Maple, Birch Faced Plywood
photo by Peter Cook

◎ このレストランは午前11時から真夜中まで、食事、酒、お茶をだす大衆的な食事の場としてデザインされた。客席は食事エリアに100席あり、酒を飲んだり、テーブルを待つ人を25人まで収容できるバーがそれを補っている。

◎ 内部のスペースは1960年代のブロックで設計された脊相な建物の中にあり、建物の正面は手入れが悪かったため、傷みのひどい状態になっていた。場所は、ウエストエンドと入口密度が高い住居地区で、大ロンドンの中心にある、人出の多い街路に面した所である。明確で簡素なインテリア組織をつくりだす必要は別にして、レストランの存在と利用しやすさが何よりも重要だと考えられた。街路と内部スペースの間に極めて透明なファサード・スクリーンを入れる設計をすることになったのは、ストリート・ミーン内に近づきやすい積極的な存在をつくりだしたいという願いからで、上の建物の全体的なみにくさから気をそらさせる必要もそれに結びついていた。こうして、外部と内部の全体の視覚的コンタクトが、この仕掛けを使って、ロンドンの気候のせいで他のヨーロッパ都市でやっているようにカフェが舗道にまでだせない欠点をカバーするのである。

This restaurant has been designed as a 'popular' dining place serving meals, drinks and teas from eleven in the morning through to midnight. It seats 100 people in the dining area and is complemented by a bar which accommodates up to 25 people drinking and waiting for tables.

This interior space is housed within a poorly designed 1960's block, whose main elevation has suffered from a lack of maintenance over the intervening years. The location is, however, on a busy street in a major London centre, between the west end and a densely populated residential quarter. Apart from the need to create a clear and simple interior organization it was felt that the accessibility and presence of the restaurant was all-important. It was this desire to create an accessible and positive presence within the street scene, combined with the need to distract from the general ugliness of the building above that led to the design of a highly transparent facade screen between the street and the interior space. Thus total visual contact between outside and inside is achieved by means of this device where, owing to the London climate, 'cafe life' can hardly flow out onto the pavement as it does in other European cities.

bar

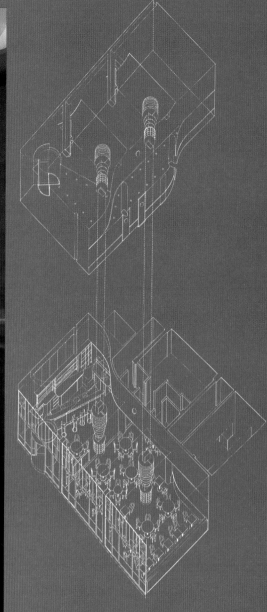

restaurant

front facade

# WILLIAM ALSOP + JOHN LYALL ARCHITECTS
## ウィリアム・アルソップ + ジョン・ライアル・アーキテクツ

P : Swimming Pool
T : Sheringham Leisure Pool, "The Splash"
D : William Alsop + John Lyall Collaboration:
    Peter Clash and Mike Waddington
C : North Norfolk District Council/Clifford
    Barnett Developments, Waddington
L : North Norfolk
A : 2,300m²
M : Soft Wood, Stained Plywood, Aluminium
photo by Ian Lambot

◎プロジェクトの目的は特別な乗物マシンなどが
あるレジャー・プールと大きな公共のドライ・エ
リアのために、同種の建物でかかる費用のほぼ半
額の予算で高品質の設計を提供することであった。

The purpose of the project was to provide a high quality design for a leisure pool with special rides wave machine etc. and large public dry areas for a budget of roughly half the price such buildings otherwise cost.

exterior

pool interior

across pool

poolside

P : Ferry Terminal
T : Hamburg Ferry Terminal
D : William Alsop | John Lyall Architects with
    Jonathan Adams, Andrea Marx＋Medium
    Architekten Hamburg
C : DFDS Seaways
L : Hamburg
A : 10,000m²
M : Precast Concrete, Glass, Translucent
    Polycarbonate, Polished Aluminium, Zinc
    Sheeting
photo by Sectional Model of Project

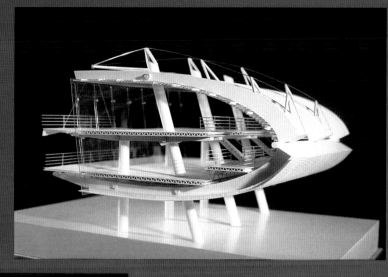

◎フェリー・ターミナル・プロジェクトはハンブルク市都市計画局が主催し、船会社のDFDSシーウェイズが後援したコンペティションの優勝作品であった。

◎建物は3つの面をもって建てられ、フェリーとクルーザー船のための埠頭施設を用意することになった。建物は2種のタイプからなる──絶えずカーブする部分の建物には旅客用施設のすべてと、乗船・下船システムが入っている。この建物部に小さなオフィスとサービス・ボックスが付属している。

◎建物は脚の上にのっていて、いつも敷地を浸す満潮の水面の上に出るようになっていて、下で車をまわすことができる。

The ferry terminal project was the winner of a competition set by the Hamburg City Planning Department and sponsored by the shipping company DFDS Seaways.
The building will be built in 3 phases and will provide landing facilities for ferries and cruser ships.
The buildings are of two types, a continuous curved section building houses all the passenger facilities and embarking/alighting systems, this building is attatched to small office and service boxes to the rear.
The buildings are raised on legs to lift them above the flooding that regularly covers the site and to allow vehicle circulation beneath.

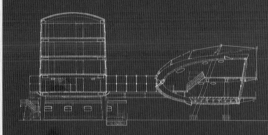

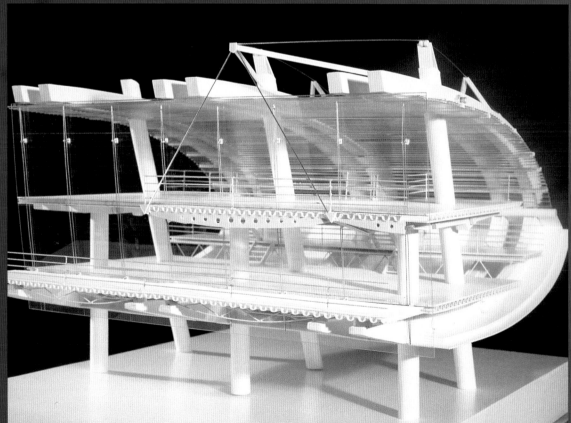

P : Exhibition Pavilion
T : UK. Pavilion, Seville World Exhibition
D : Will Alsop＋John Lyall, Collaboration:
    Johnathan Adams, Holger Jaedicke＋Simon
    North
C : UK. Governmint, Department of Trade and
    Industry
L : Seville, Spain
A : 7,000m²
M : British Hard and Softwood, Steel, Glass

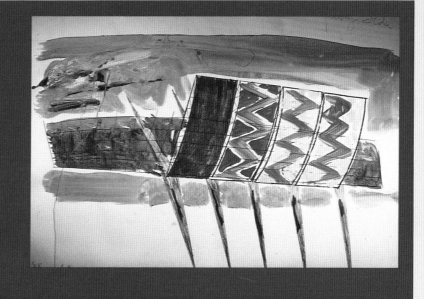

◎ この企画は英連邦政府の通商産業省主催の招待コンペティションのためにデザインされた。企画は一連のフレキシブルなギャラリーと経験的なゾーンを通る、豪華なプロムナード、機会のマトリックスである。パビリオンは総合的な気候のコントロール装置（飛行船とウォター・ウォールを含む）のシステムを使い、それら装置もまた展示の一部をなしている。

The scheme was designed for invited
competition set by the U.K. Governments
Dept. of Trade and Industry.
The scheme is a spectacular promenade
through a series of flexible galleries and
experiential zones; a matrix of
opportunities. The pavilion uses a system
of integrated climatic control devises
(including an airship and a water wall)
which are all also part of the exhibition.

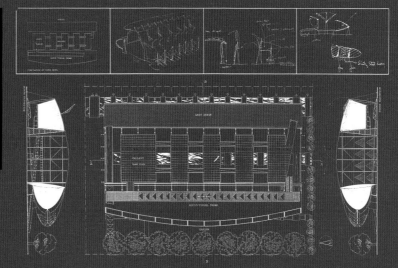

perspective view

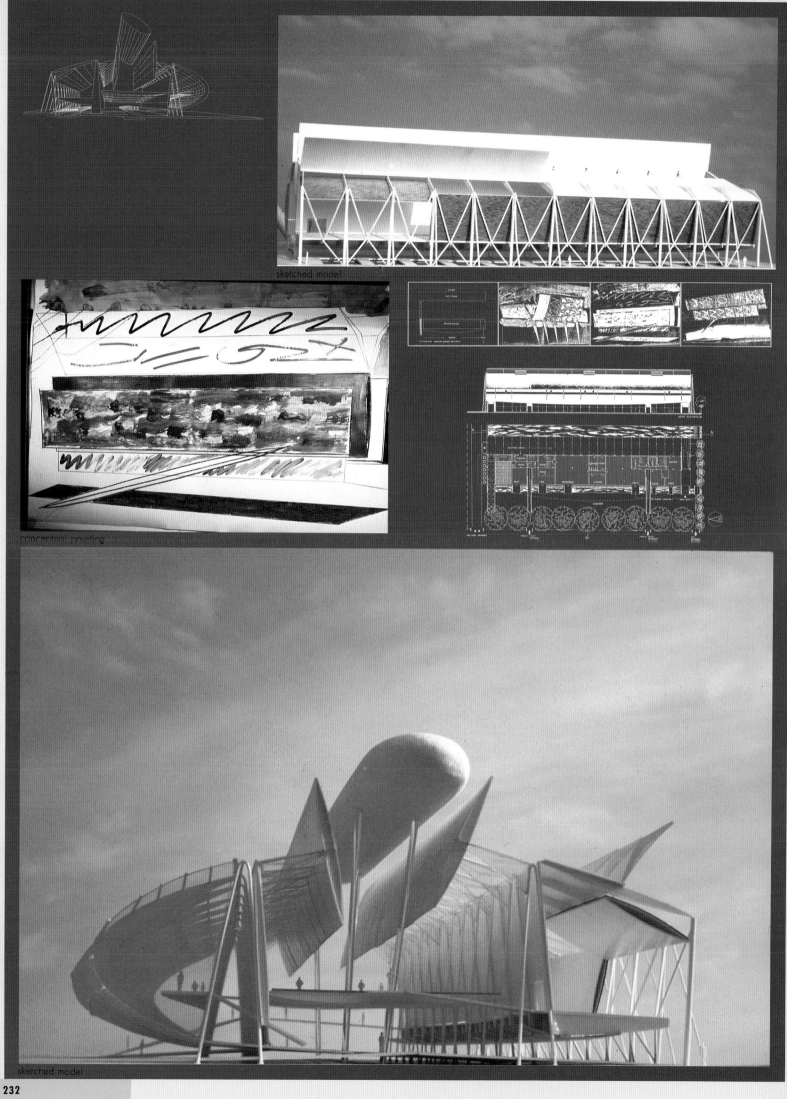

sketched model

conceptual painting

sketched model

P : Housing and Workplace
T : Hafenstarsse
D : William Alsop＋John Lyall Collaboration:
    Jonathan Adams, Simon North
C : City of Hamburg Planning Department
L : Hamburg
A : 9,000m²
M : Concrete Structure, Glass, Steel Plate

◎ このプロジェクトはハンブルクの不景気な地域を再生させることを目的とした。それは単身者と小家族向けの公共住宅と、小規模事業のためのワークショップ、スタジオとからなる。

◎ 建物は 2 本の進路、1 本は他方より 9 ｍ高いが、その間の敷地いっぱいに建つ。2 つのブロックに分かれ、低いブロックにはワークショップ、高いブロックには住宅が入る。

This project is intended to revitalize a depreesed area of Hamburg. It consists of public housing for single people and small famillies, and workshop/studios for small businesses.
The building fills a site between 2 roads, one road being 9m above the other. It is diveded into 2 block the lower block containing workshops and the upper block the housing.

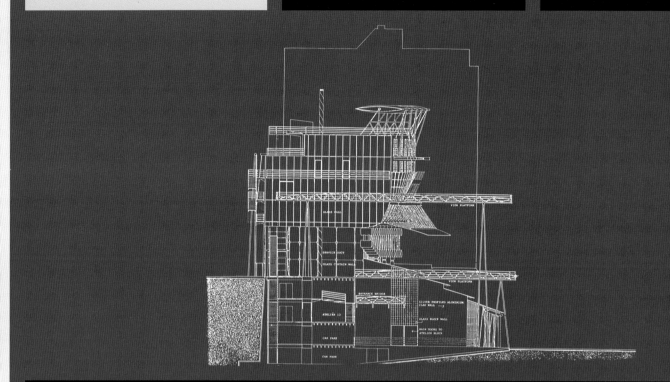

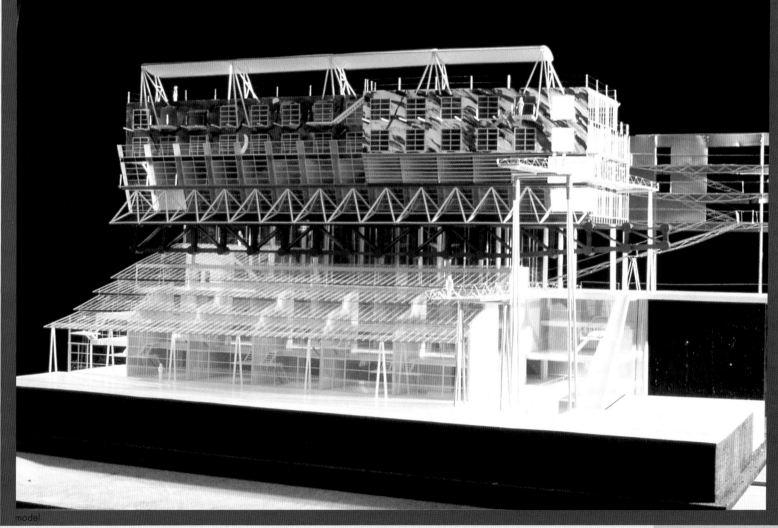

model

model

sketch model

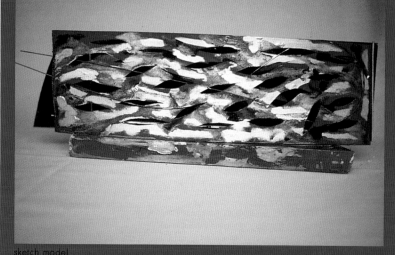

sketch model

conceptual painting

# ZAHA HADID
## ザハ・ハデイド

P : New Development
T : Tomigaya
D : Zaha M.Hadid
C : K1 Corporation
L : Tokyo
M : Concrete, Glass

◎この建物の敷地と通りに対する関係は過密な都市にあっては異例のものである。軽量ガラスのパビリオンが建てられて、小さな都会の真空地帯をつくりだし、周囲の環境の喧騒からの救いを用意してくれる。この何もない空間は2つの水平面の間に吊される圧縮されたスペースである。

◎プログラムの主要部は湾曲する1階の床の下に沈められている。1階の床は2つの側面で縁から引き戻され、光を下のスペースに透過させるチャンネルの中で、高いガラス壁を支える。入口の階段は中間レベルのプラットホームと下のスペース内の外のコートへ降りていく。ここではグラウンド・レベルを通って上方の別のプラットホームと上のパビリオンの腹部を眺めることができる。下のスペースのゆったりした比率が、1つの連続するスペースか、または一連のプラットホームとして、完全なフレキシビリティーを可能にし、このスペースを小売やオフィス活動に使わせてくれる。

◎高く持ち上げられたパビリオンは、完全に独立しているが、建物全体のコンセプトのなかで絶対必要な一部である。それは軽い1階の構造で開いた地面の上に浮かび、湾曲したルーフ・ラインと3面に上から下までの窓をもつ。デザインはオフィス、スタジオ、または小売用としてフレキシビリティーを与える。

interior model

The relationship of this building to the site and the street is an unusual one is a crowded city. A light glass pavilion is elevated to create a small urban void, providing relief from the clutter of the surrounding neighbourhood. This void is a compressed space suspended between two horizontal planes.

A major part of the program is sunk below the curving first floor which is pulled back from the edges on two sides and holds a tall glass wall in a channel which allows light to filter into the lower space. The entrance stairway steps down to a mid-level platform and an external court within the lower space. This provides view up past the ground level to another platform and the belly of the pavilion above. The generous proportions the lower space enable complete flexibility, as either one continuous floor or a series of platforms, allowing this space to be used for retail and office activities.

The raised pavilion, although completely independent, is an integral part of the whole building concept. It is a light, one-story structure which hovers above the open ground, with a curving roof line and full height windows on three sides. The design offers flexibility for office, studio or retail use.

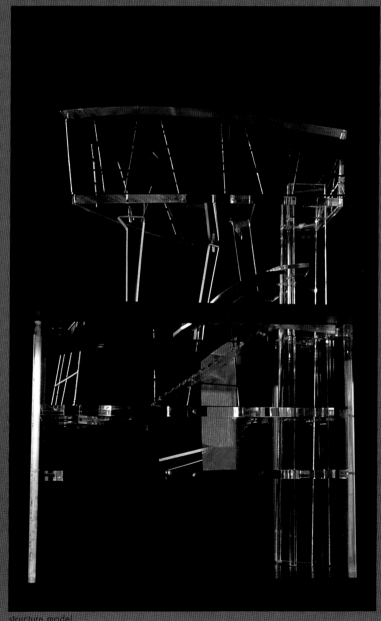
structure model

presentation

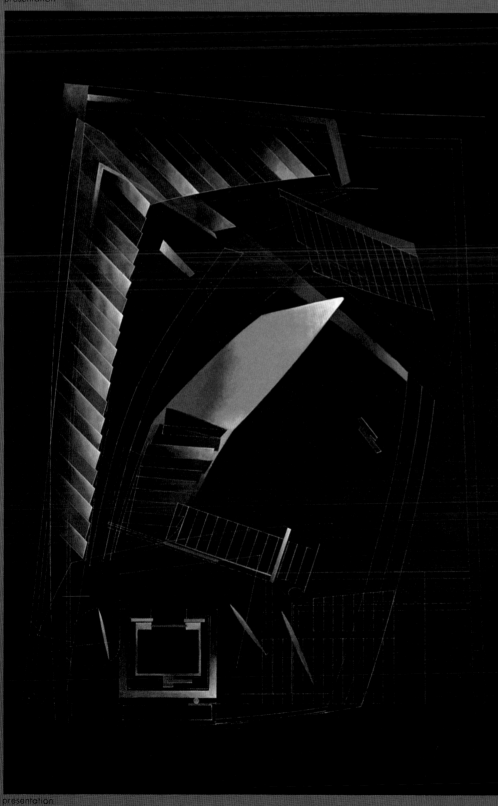

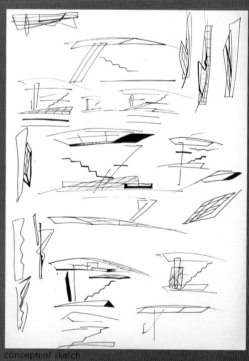

conceptual sketch

presentation

P : Offices
T : Kurfurstendamm
D : Zaha M.Hadid
L : Berlin
M : Aluminium, Glass, Coucrete

◎建物のプランは弓のように曲がり、ゆるやかにカーブして隅のほうに向かい、各階が少しずつ大きくなっていく。こうして建物は断面の最上部で、平面図では隅で、最大の建坪となる。この配置はオフィスにできるフロア・エリアを最大にしないが、オフィス・スペースにダイナミックな質を生みだす。そのスペースは各階で少しずつ大きさと形を変え、同じフロアを繰り返すという、オフィス・ブロックの通常の状態を否定する。オフィス・フロア・エリアには、まだプロジェクトの制限のなかで効率よく機能するのに十分な広さがあり、類例のないスペースの質からして高い賃貸料が見込めるので、フロア・エリアが狭くなるという損失を相殺するだろう。
◎建物の壁は屋根の上まで立ち上げられて、屋根を戸外の、空に向かって開いた部屋にして、限られているとはいえ、外やアデナウアー・プラッツが見える。

The plan of the building is bowed and gently curved and moves out toward the corner, becoming slightly larger on each floor. The building thus reaches the maximum building site at its top in section, and the corner in plan.
This arrangement, though not maximizing the possible floor area of the offices creates a dynamic quality in the office spaces, which consequently change slightly in size and shape on each floor, denying the normal condition in an office block of the repetition of identical floors. The office floor areas are still large enough to function efficiently within the constraints of the project, and the exceptional quality of the spaces will allow for higher rents to offset the losses of smaller floor areas.
The walls of the building are brought up above the roof to allow the roof to become an outdoor room, open to the sky, with controlled, limited views out and across Adenauer Platz.

model

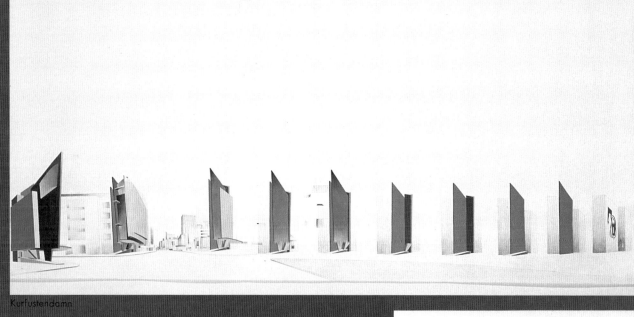

Kurfustendamn

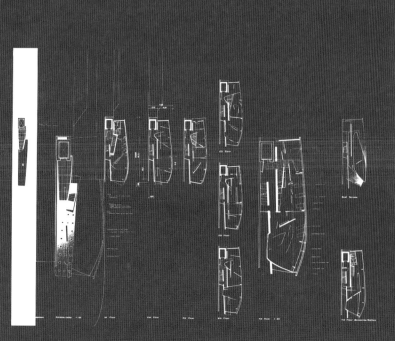

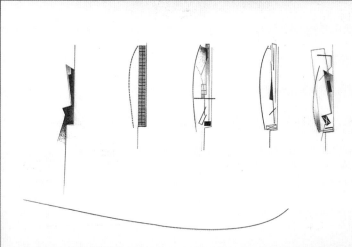

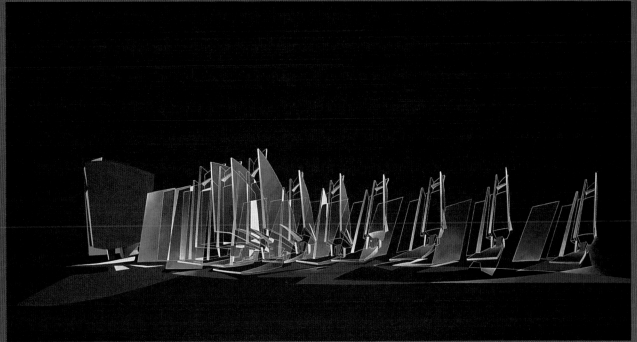

presentation

P : Shop
T : Azabu-Jyuban
D : Zaha M.Hadid
C : K1 Corporation
L : Tokyo

◎ この清潔なガラスの建物は周囲の手当たりしだいに建てられた環境を、清潔で鋭い稜で切り取っている。建物は様々な機能を独立のスペースに圧縮し、その関連するスペースの特質を用いてそれぞれの用途を定義してつくられた。湾曲したエントランス・ランプは上や下から建物を奥まで見せてくれる。空中に開いたこの新しい舗道は建物の中心部まで通じていて、通りから進んでいくにつれて内部が徐々に姿を現す。ひとたび建物の中心部に到ると、垂直の階段が建物の上まで通じており、それが突然開いてゆったりしたバルコニーや床と床の中間にある踊場となっている。この階段は異なるレベルのスペースをのぞかせてくれ、繊細なガラスの壁が各スペースに光を入れている。

This pristine glass building cuts a clean sharp edge through the randomly built environment of the surrounding area. The building is formed by compressing various functions into independent spaces, and using the character of their related spaces to define each use. The curving entrance ramp offers views below and above into the depths of the building. This new pavement, open to the air, leads into the heart of the building, which slowly reveals itself during the passage form the street.
Once in the heart of the building a vertical stairway runs up the entire height of the building which breaks out forming generous balconies and mid-floor landings. This stairway gives glimpses through to spaces on many different levels, with the delicate glass wall bringing light into each space.

interior

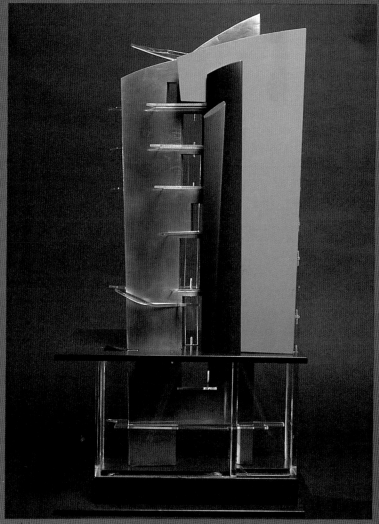

model

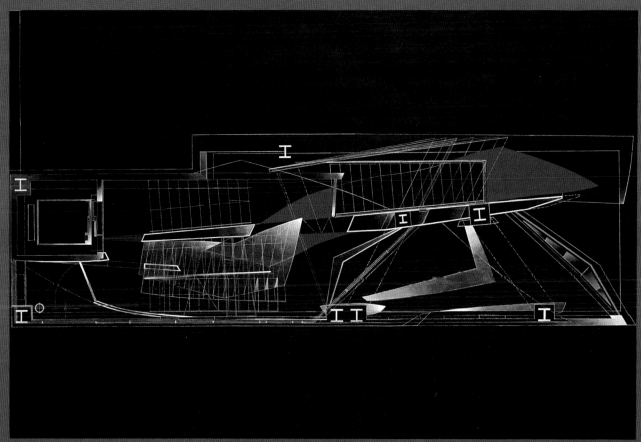

elevation

building

## ANDREW HOLMES
### アンドルー・ホームズ

18···22

address : 27 Leigh Road London N5 1AH

phone : 01-226-2687

◎ Born in Worcestershire, England, in 1947, Andrew Holmes was a member of the Architectural Association between 1966 and 1972. In 1972 he took the first prize for "The City as a Significant Enviroment" award, and in 1974 the first prize for the RIBA/Rotring Architectural Drawings award in 1974. In addition to this he has collected the D and AD Silver Award from the Penguin Book of Kites, and between 1980 and 1982 worked on the invention and design of the new Bus Map for London Transport. He has worked as an architect, and interior designer and a graphic artist since 1974, and became Unit Master of the Architectural Association, London, in 1985. He has taken part in several public and private collections, including the RIBA Drawings Collection.

◎ 1947年、イギリスのウースターシャーに生まれたアンドルー・ホームズは、1966年から1972年まで建築協会のメンバーであった。1972年「重要な環境としての都市」賞を受賞。1974年度リバ／ロットリング建築ドローイング賞を受賞。この他にペンギン社の凧の本からDおよびADシルバー賞を受賞した。1980年から1982年にかけロンドン交通機関のため新しいバス地図を案出し、デザインした。1974年以来建築家、インテリア・デザイナーそしてグラフィック・デザイナーとして活躍している。1985年にはロンドンの建築協会のユニット・マスターとなった。彼はリバ・ドローイング・コレクションを含む、いくつかの公的、私的コレクションに参加している。

## ARCHITEKTURBURO BOLLES WILSON
### アーキテクトゥルビュロー・ボレス・ウィルソン

23···30

address : 5 Thurloe Square London SW7 2TA

phone : 01-589-7560

◎ Peter Wilson was the Unit Master of the AA Diploma School Unit 1 between1978 and 1988, and has been in practice with Julia Bolles Wilson as the Wilson Partnership since 1980. Their winning entry in the recent competition for the Munster city library was featured in AA Files No.14. They also completed Blackburn House, Hampstead, London, in 1988 and are currently working on projects in Germany and Japan.

◎ ピーター・ウィルソンは1978年から1988年にかけて、AAディプロマ・スクール・ユニット1のユニット・マスターであった。そして1980年以来、ジュリア・ボレス・ウィルソンとウィルソン合名会社をつくって仕事をしている。2人がミュンスター市立図書館のため最近行われたコンペティションに優勝し、このことは、AAファイルス14号の特集となった。2人は1988年に、ロンドン、ハムステッドのブラックバーン・ハウスを完成し、現在西ドイツと日本でのプロジェクトに従事している。

## ARMSTRONG ASSOCIATES
### アームストロング・アソシエーツ

31···37

address : 2 Hinde Street London W1M 5RN

phone : 01-935-6389

◎ Kenneth Armstrong trained at the Mackintosh Shool in Glasgow and the Royal College of Art, London, and subsequently worked at Foster Associates where he was involved primarily with the Hong Kong & Shanghai Bank and the winning BBC Competition entry. Before setting up Armstrong Chipperfield in 1984 he worked for DEGW as team coordinator on the feasibility study for the Barclays Bank Headquarters at Radbroke Hall. He has also taught at the Bartlett School of Architecture and lectured at the Royal College of Art.

## BEEVOR+MULL ASSOCIATES
### ビーヴァ+マル・アソシエーツ

38···44

address : 17 Leathermarket Street London SE1 3HN

phone : 01-407-1346

◎ Catrina and Robert first met in 1983; their final year at the A.A. in Nigel Coates' Unit 10. After graduation they co-founded the NATO group which wrote and published manifestos under this same name. They have also run their own architectural practice since 1984. They started off on small projects, mainly working for their circle of friends, but soon expanded their business to larger scale projects for private and commercial concerns. However, Beevor+Mull have no intentions of over-expanding the business as their personal contact with suppliers and clients is their trade-mark and of this they are rightly proud. They are currently working on a restaurant, a bar in West London, a warehouse/studio and a private house abroad.

◎ カトリナとロバートは1983年、つまりナイジェル・コーツのユニット10のAAにおける最終学年のときに出会った。卒業後、2人は共同でNATOグループを創立し、NATOグループはこの名前で宣言文を書いて発表した。また2人は1984年以来自分たち自身の建築事務所を経営している。最初は主に友人たちのサークルのための仕事をする、小さなプロジェクトとして出発した。しかしほどなく事業を広げて、個人や営利企業のための比較的大規模なプロジェクトにたずさわるようになった。しかし、ビーヴァ+マルは業者やクライアントとの個人的なつながりが彼らのトレードマークであり、このことを誇りにしていたので、事業を過度に拡張する意図がなかった。彼らは現在ロンドン西部で、レストランとバー、海外で倉庫、スタジオと個人の家等をつくっている。

◎ ケネス・アームストロングはグラスゴーのマッキントッシュ・スクールと、ロンドンのロイヤル・カレッジ・オブ・アートで教育を受け、その後フォスター・アソシエーツで働き、主として香港&上海銀行、そしてBBCコンペティションに参加優勝作品に関係してきた。1984年にアームストロング・チッパーフィールドを設立する前は、DEGWのためチーム共同コーディネーターとして働き、ラドブローク・ホールのバークレイズ銀行本部のフィージビリティ・スタディに従事した。またバートレット・スクール・オブ・アーキテクチュアで教え、ロイヤル・カレッジ・オブ・アートで講義したこともある。

## BEN KELLY DESIGN
### ベン・ケリー・デザイン

45...50

address : 3 Errol Street London EC1Y
        8LX

phone : 01-628-6935

◎ Ben Kelly was born in Welwyn Garden City in 1949 and attended the Lancaster School of Art between 1966 and 1970 before going onto the Royal College of Art (1971-1974) where he obtained an MA and RCA. Building up work experience between 1974 and 1976, he opened Ben Kelly Design in November '76.

◎ ベン・ケリーは1949年ウェルウィン・ガーデン・シティで生まれ、1966年から1970年までランカスター・スクール・オブ・アートで学び、その後ロイヤル・カレッジ・オブ・アートに移り(1971〜1974)、そこで修士号とRCAを取った。1974年から1976年にかけて実務の経験を積み、1976年11月ベン・ケリー・デザインを開いた。

## BENSON+FORSYTH
### ベンソン+フォーサイス

51...54

address : 37d Mildmay Grove London
        N1 4RH

phone : 01-359-0288

◎ Professor Gordon Benson was born in Glasgow in 1944, and Alan Forsyth in Newcastle Upon Tyne in the same year. They both graduated from the Architectural Association School of Artchitecture in 1968 and set up a private practice together in 1978. Featuring strongly in various international competitions. they have completed many succesful projects from housing estates to the Pavilion for the Glasgow Garden Festival. Work they are currently involved in includes a Science Market and a commercial development in Glasgow. In addition to running the partnership, they are also both involved in academic teaching roles.

◎ ゴードン・ベンソン教授は1949年グラスゴーで、アラン・フォーサイスは同じ年ニューカッスル・アポン・タインで生まれた。両人とも1968年に、アーキテクチュラル・アソシエーション・スクール・オブ・アーキテクチュアを卒業し、1978年ともに個人事務所を設立した。さまざまな国際的コンペティションで頭角を現し、住宅団地からグラスゴー・ガーデン・フェスティヴァルのパビリオンまで多くのプロジェクトを手がけて成功させている。彼らが現在たずさわっている仕事は、グラスゴーでのサイエンス・マーケットと商業開発である。合名会社を経営するばかりでなく、両人とも専門の教育にもたずさわっている。

## BRANSON COATES ARCHITECTURE
### ブランソン・コーツ・アーキテクチュア

55...59

address : 23 Old Street London EC1

phone : 01-490-0343

◎ Born in Malvern, England, in 1949, Coates graduated from the Nottingham University in 1971 with and honours degree architecture. A member of the Architectural Association between 1974 and 1978, Coats also won a scholarship sponsored by the Italian Government to the Rome University in 1978. His teaching experience spans almost two decades with positions at the Bennington College, Vermont, between 1970 and 1981, and Unit Master of the Diploma Unit 10 at the Architectural Association from 1977 to the present day. One of the founders of NATO (Narrative Architecture Today), Coates formed Branson Coates Architecture with Doug Branson in 1985.

◎ 1949年イギリスのマルヴァーンに生まれたコーツは1971年、ノッティンガム大学の建築学部を優等で卒業した。1974年から1978年までアーキテクチュラル・アソシエーションのメンバーであり、1978年にイタリア政府が後援するローマ大学への奨学金を獲得した。教師としては20年におよぶ経験があり、1970年から1981年までヴァーモントのベニングトン・カレッジで、1977年から現在までアーキテクチュラル・アソシエーションのデプロマ・ユニット10で教えている。NATO(今日の叙事的建築)の創立メンバーの1人で、1985年ダグ・ブランソンと、ブランソン・コーツ・アーキテクチュアをつくった。

## CAMPBELL ZOGOLOVITCH WILKINSON+GOUGH
### キャンベル・ゾゴロヴィッチ・ウィルキンソン+ゴフ

60...67

address : 17 Bowling Green Lane
        London EC1R 0BD

phone : 01-253-2523

◎ Nick Campbell, Roger Zogolovitch, Rex Wilkinson and Piers Gough all trained together at the Architectural Association School in London in the late sixties. They set up their first office in the basement of the school and concentrated on the design of swinging boutiques and private house alterations. The actual partnership (CZWG) was formed in 1975, and much of their early work was conversions. They are now involved in a wide range of new-build projects, and their office has expanded to 45 staff members.

◎ ニック・キャンベル、ロジャー・ゾゴロヴィッチ、レクス・ウィルキンソンおよびピアス・ゴフはともに1960年代の後半、ロンドンのアーキテクチュラル・アソシエーション・スクールで教育を受けた。彼らは最初の事務所を母校の地下室で開き、流行の先端をいくブティックや個人住宅の改造に力を注いだ。実際に共同事務所を組織(CZWG)したのは1975年で、初期の仕事の多くは改造であった。現在、彼らは、広い範囲にわたる新築プロジェクトに専心しており、事務所は45人のスタッフを抱えるまでになった。

## CASSON MANN DESIGNERS
カッソン・マン・デザイナーズ

68...74

address : 14 Cornwall Crescent London W11 1PP

phone : 01-727-6866

◎ Dinah Casson and Roger Mann formed thier partnership in 1984. They remain a small practice which is well-known for its close collaboration with other designers, architects and project managers. Although mostly concerned with interior, exhibition and furniture design, one of their major projects has been the successful corperate indentity and shop design of Grangelato Ice-cream. They are currently involved in the design of a major exhibition of the new British Design to be held in Boymans Museum, Rotterdam, for the FCO. In addition to running the partnership, both also operate as visiting lecturers for the Kingston Polytechnic (Roger Mann) and the Royal College of Art (Dinah Casson). Ms. Casson was also a member of the Design Council between 1982 and 1988.

◎ ダイナ・カッソンとロジャー・マンは1984年に共同事務所を設立した。2人は小さい事務所のままで、他のデザイナー、建築家やプロジェクト・マネージャーとの関係が密接なことで知られている。多くはインテリア、展示、家具のデザインに関した仕事だが、主なプロジェクトのひとつは、グランジェラート・アイスクリームのコーポレート・アイデンティティとショップ・デザインであり、成功を収めた。現在2人はFCOのため、ロッテルダムのボイマンズ博物館で催される新しいブリティッシュ・デザインという大きな展覧会のデザインに専念している。共同で事務所を経営するほか、2人は客員講師の職にもついており、ロジャー・マンはキングストン・ポリテクニックで、ダイナ・カッソンはロイヤル・カレッジ・オブ・アートで教えている。カッソン女史は1982年から1988年まで、デザイン・カウンシルのメンバーでもあった。

## DAVID CHIPPERFIELD + PARTNERS
ディヴィッド・チッパーフィールド・パートナーズ

91...96

address : 142-144 New Cavendish Street London W1M 7FG

phone : 01-255-2888

◎ David Chipperfield trained at the Architectural Association and during his career has worked for several major practices. Chipperfield Associates was founded in 1984 and focused on designorientated work in the UK and abroad. The firm established a reputation through a series of shop interiors, and has expanded to larger

## COOK + HAWLEY ARCHITECTS
クック＋ホーレイ・アーキテクツ

75...84

address : 12 Ladbroke Square London W11 3NA

phone : 01-727-6884

◎ Christine Hawley was born in Shrewsbury in 1949 and has a long and distinguished teaching career. She was appointed head of the Architectural School of the Northeast London Polytechnic (NELP) in 1987 which made her not only the first women ever to head a British school of architecture, but also the yungest head (a position she still holds).

◎ Peter Cook was born in Southend-on Sea in 1936 and is presently the head of the Architecture Department of the "Stadtelschule" (State Art Academy) in Frankfurt. A guest professor at several universities throughout the world, Peter Cook is alao a prolific writer who has written several books and numerous magazine articles.

◎ The partnership between Christine Hawley and Peter Cook was established in 1977, and they are currently working on a housing block in Berlin as part of the IBA and another housing block in Kensington, London.

◎ クリスティン・ホーレイは1942年シュールズベリーに生まれ、長く教職についていて優れた業績がある。彼女は1987年ノースイースト・ロンドン・ポリテクニック（NELP）の校長を務めた。イギリスの建築学校で校長になった最初の女性であるとともに、最年少の校長でもあった（現在も在職）。

◎ ピーター・クックは1963年、サウスエンド・オン・シーで生まれ、現在はフランクフルトにある「シュタッテルシューレ」（国立アート・アカデミー）の建築学部の学部長である。世界各地の大学の客員教授をしており、また数冊の著書や多数の雑誌に記事を書き、多数の著作がある。

◎ クリスティン・ホーレイとピーター・クックの共同事務所は1977年に開設され、現在はIBAの一部としてのベルリンの住宅ブロックと、別にロンドンのケンジントンでの住宅ブロックの仕事に従事している。

scale work. Current projects include urban design projects in London, a private museum in Tokyo, a hotel and health clcub in Yokohama and a studio complex in London. David Chipperfield was a founding memver of the 9H Gallery, and has also taught extensively including a present position as visiting professor at Harvard University.

◎ ディヴィッド・チッパーフィールドはアーキテクチュラル・アソシエーションで教育を受け、そ

## DANIEL WEIL + GERARD TAYLOR
ダニエル・ワイル＋ジェラルド・テーラー

85...90

address : 3 Plough Yard London EC2A 3LP

phone : 01-247-5628

◎ Daniel Weil was born in Buenos Aires, Argentina in 1953. He graduated in architecture from the University of Buenos Aires in 1977 and then moved to London to continue his studies at the Royal College of Art. He graduated in 1981 and started his own electronics manufacturing company, Parenthesis Linmited. Between 1983 and 1985 he was unit master at the Architectural Association with Nigel Coates.

◎ Gerard Taylor was born in Glasgow, Scotland in 1955 and studied design at the Glasgow School of Art before graduating in industrial design from the Royal College of Art. After working for the BBC, he moved to Milan where he worked with Sottsass Associati from 1982 until 1985. Daniel Weil Gerard Taylor was established in 1985 and since then they have worked areas of interior architecture, retail design, industrial design and furniture design for clients in the UK, Europe, America and Japan.

◎ ダニエル・ワイルは1953年にアルゼンチンのブエノスアイレスで生まれた。1977年のブエノスアイレス大学を卒業し、その後ロンドンに移ってロイヤル・カレッジ・オブ・アートで勉学を続けた。1981年に卒業して、自分自身のエレクトロニクス製造会社、パレンセシス株式会社を設立。1983年から1985年までナイジェル・コーツとともに、アーキテクチュラル・アソシエーションのユニット・マスターを勤めた。

◎ ジェラルド・テーラーは1955年、スコットランドのグラスゴーで生まれ、グラスゴー・スクール・オブ・アートでデザインを学び、その後ロイヤル・カレッジ・オブ・アートのインダストリアル・デザイン科を卒業した。BBCのために働いたあと、ミラノに移り、1982年から1985年までソッツアス・アソシアーティで働いた。ダニエル・ワイル・ジェラルド・テーラーは1985年に設立され、以来2人は英連邦、ヨーロッパ、アメリカおよび日本のクライアントのために、インテリア・アーキテクチュア、小売店デザイン、インダストリアル・デザインおよび家具デザインの分野で活動している。

の後いくつかの大きな仕事をやってきた。チッパーフィールド・アソシエーツを1984年に設立し、英連邦と海外でのデザインの仕事に専念してきた。会社は一連の店舗デザインによって地位を確立し、大規模な仕事に手を広げるようになった。現在のプロジェクトにはロンドンの市街地デザイン・プロジェクト、東京の私設博物館、横浜のホテル兼ヘルスクラブおよびロンドンのスタジオ・コンプレックスなどがある。ディヴィッド・チッパーフィールドは9Hギャラリーの創立メンバーであった。現在、ハーバード大学での客員教授など、広く教育に当たっている。

## DIN ASSOCIATES
ディン・アソシエーツ

102...110

address : 6 South Lambeth Place London
SW8 1SP

phone : 01-582-0777

◎ Rasshied Ali Din was born in April 1956 and studied at the Birmingham Polytechnic between 1975 and 1979. He worked for three of the UK's top design consultancies before setting up Din Associates in February 1986. The amount of projects completed within 1988 stretches into double figures and includes an impressive list of shops and department stores, boardrooms and a conference centre.

◎ ラシード・アリ・ディンは1956年4月に生まれ、1975年から1979年まで、バーミンガム・ポリテクニックで学んだ。英連邦で一流のデザイン・コンサルタント社、3社で働いたあと、1986年2月ディン・アソシエーツを設立。1988年内に完成したプロジェクトの統計は2桁台の数字に伸び、店舗、デパート、会議室、会議センターなどのリストは見事である。

## EVA JIRICNA ARCHITECTS
エヴァ・ジリクナ・アーキテクツ

116...124

address : 7 Dering Street London W1R
9AB

phone : 01-629-7077

◎ Eva Jiricna qualified as an engineer/ architect at the University of Prague in 1962 and recieved a postgraduate degree from the Prague Academy of Fine Arts in 1963. She came to the UK in 1968 and worked for a year with the GLC schools' division before becoming an associate with Louis de Soissons Partnership, working on the planning, design and construction programmes for Brighton Marina. She set up her own practice in 1980 with David Hodges and formed Jiricna Kerr Associates in 1985.

◎ エヴァ・ジリクナは1962年プラハ大学で技師／建築家の資格を取り、1963年プラハ・アカデミー・オブ・ファイン・アーツで大学院の学位を得た。1968年に英連邦に来てGLC・スクール部門で1年間働いたあと、ルイ・ド・ソワソンズ・パートナーシップに加わり、ブライトン・マリーナのための計画、設計、建設プログラムに従事した。1980年ディヴィッド・ホッジズとともに、彼女自身の事務所を設立し、1985年ジリクナ・アーキテクツをつくった。

## D'SOTO '88 DESIGN GROUP
デ・ソト '88 デザイン・グループ

111...115

address : The Engine Room North
Buildings, Spring House 10
Spring Place London NW5
3BH

phone : 01-267-2449

◎ Jose Cruzat-Salazar, Ron Brinkers and Ric Zito all studied together as students of Architecture and Design Kingston Polytechnic and officially set up D'Soto '88 in June 1987. They work in various areas of design including architecture, interiors, exhibition work and also set design for photographic and graphic design. Their distinctive style stems from several different influences, but it is their own insrpiration and enthusiasm for articulated engineering that gives dynamic expression of technology to their work. A common feature of D'Soto's work is visually celebrated junctions and fixings.

◎ ジョウゼ・クルザット・ザラザール、ロン・ブリンカーズおよびリック・ジットはみな一緒にキングストン・ポリテクニックで建築とデザイン科の学生として学び、1987年6月正式にデ・ソト'88を設立。彼らは建築やインテリアや展示作業などさまざまな分野で活躍し、同時に写真のデザインやグラフィックデザインも行う。彼ら独特のスタイルはいくつかの別々な影響力から出たものだが、その作品にテクノロジーのダイナミックな表現を与えているのは、彼ら自身のインスピレーションと関連工学に対する情熱である。デ・ソトの作品に共通する特色は視覚的な接合と取付けである。

◎ 1977年にキングストン・ポリテクニックを3Dで卒業して以来、ディヴィッド・ディヴィスはTVグラフィックスの仕事を続け、コンラン・アソシエーツでグラフィック・デザインとアートのシニア・ディレクターになった。1982年、ディヴィッド・ディヴィス・アソシエーツを設立して、80人のスタッフを抱え、年に600万ポンド以上の売上げをもち、英連邦第一のデザイン・コンサルタント社に育て上げた。設立当初から、DDAはネクスト、ブリティッシュ・エアウエイズ、マークス&スペンサー、バートン・グループおよびミッドランド・バンクのような依頼者のための大きなプロジェクトに専念することにより、時代のトレンドを先取りする力となってきた。また彼はロンドンでプロダクション会社と小売店も始めた。

## FOSTER ASSOCIATES
フォスター・アソシエーツ

135...146

address : 172-182 Great Portland Street
London W1N 5TB

phone : 01-637-5431

◎ Norman Foster was born in Manchester in 1935 and studied both Architecture and City Planning at Manchester University. He graduated in 1961 and was awarded a Henry Fellowship to Yale University where he received a Masters Degree in Architecture. He returned to the UK in 1963, and set up the Foster Associates with Wendy Foster in 1967. He worked with Buckminster Fuller on a number of projects between 1968 and 1983. Norman Foster was awarded the Royal Gold Medal for Architecture in 1983.

◎ ノーマン・フォスターは1935年マンチェスターで生まれ、マンチェスター大学で建築と都市計画の両方を学んだ。1961年に卒業して、エール大学のヘンリー・フェローシップを授与されて、エール大で建築の修士号を取った。1963年英連邦にもどり、1967年ウェンディ・フォスターとフォスター・アソシエーツを設立。1968年から1983年までバックミンスター・フーラーとともに多くのプロジェクトに従事した。ノーマン・フォスターは1983年、建築家に与えられるロイヤル・ゴールド・メダルを授与された。

## DAVID DAVIES ASSOCIATES
ディヴィッド・ディヴィス・アソシエーツ

97...101

address : 12 Goslett Yard London
WC2H 0EE

phone : 01-437-9070

◎ Since graduating in 3D design from Kingston Polytechnic in 1977, Daved Davies has worked in TV graphics and was made a senior graphic design and art director at Conran Associates. He established David Davies Associates in 1982 with no external backing and has built the company up to one of the UK's top design consultancies with a staff list of 80 and an annual turnover of more than 6 million sterling. Since its beginning, DDA has been influential in derecting the trends of the decade by being involved in major projects for such clients as Next, British Airways, Marks & Spencer, the Burton Group and the Midland Bank. He has also launched a production company, DDAV, and a retail outlet in London.

## FISHER PARK LTD.
### フィッシャー・パーク・リミテッド

address : 51 Wharton Street London
         WC1X 9PA

phone : 01-837-1238

◎ Mark Fisher graduated in architecture at the Architectural Association in London. He practised as a freelance architect and in the early 70's ran the celebrated "Nice Ideas" unit at the A.A. Johnathan Park studied mechanical sciences at Clare College, Cambridge and Imperial College. London. After working with Ova Arups and Arup Associates for a number of years he set up his own engineering practice and ran Diploma Technical Studies at the A.A. Their partnership was formed in 1977 and they aimed their concentration at special effects in the world of Rock & Roll. Since then Fisher Park Limited has expanded to provide a comprehensive design service to the entertainment industry. In addition to show design, they have also covered the design of major international discoteques, leisure attractions, portable theatres and presentations for major public companies.

◎ マーク・フィッシャーはロンドンのアーキテクチュラル・アソシエーションで建築を修めた。フリーランスの建築家として仕事をし、70年代初めにAAで有名な「ナイス・アイデアズ」を経営。
◎ ジョナサン・パークはケンブリッジのクレア・カレッジとロンドンのインペリアル・カレッジで機械工学を学んだ。オヴァ・アラップス・アンド・アラップ・アソシエーツで数年働いたあと、彼自身の工学事務所を設立し、AAでディプロマ・テクニカル・スタディズを経営した。
◎ 2人の共同事務所は1977年につくられ、2人はロックンロールの世界に特別な効果を狙って力を集中した。それ以来、フィッシャー・パーク・リミテッドはエンターテイメント産業に総合的なデザイン・サービスを提供すべく、拡張をとげてきた。ショー・デザインのほかに、主な国際的なディスコやレジャー・アトラクション、主な公募会社のためのポータブル劇場やプレゼンテーションのデザインも手広くあつかってきた。

## HERRON ASSOCIATES
### ヘロン・アソシエーツ

address : Unit 24, The Turnmill 63
         Clerkenwell Road London
         EC1M 5PT

phone : 01-253-1929

◎ In a spectacular career that has stretched from 1954 when he became an architect with the Greater London Council, Ron Herron is now an major international design figure. During the early sixies he was one of the small group of architests that designed London's Heyward Gallrey and Queen Elizabeth Hall. Having worked with many of the UK's top design consultancies, he established Herron Associates in 1982. He has also held the position of tutor at the Architectual Association School in London since 1965.

◎ 1954年にグレーター・ロンドン市議会の建築家となったときに始まる数々の輝かしい経歴をもつロン・ヘロンは、現在デザイン界における国際的な大立者である。60年代初めはロンドンのヘイワード・ギャラリーとクイーン・エリザベス・ホールを設計した小さな建築家グループの一員だった。英連邦で一流のデザイン・コンサルタント社と一緒に仕事をしたあと、1982年にヘロン・アソシエーツを設立。また1965年以来、ロンドンのアーキテクチュラル・アソシエーション・スクールの講師の職にある。

## IAN RITCHIE
### イアン・リチー

address : Metropolitan Wharf Wapping
         Wall London E1

phone : 01-481-4464

◎ Ian Ritchie was born in England and trained at the Schools of Architecture in Liverpool between 1965 and 1972. He worked for Foster Associates for 4 years before setting up independantly in the UK and in France. He was one of the founder members of Chrysalis Architects, but left in 1981 to follow other interests and set up Ian Ritchie Associates in London. The firm concentrates on lightweight structes, passive solar energy, art and technology. His work has received many awards and has been widely published and exhibited. He has also lectured and taught in the UK, France and Japan.

◎ イアン・リチーはイギリスに生まれ、1965年から1972年までリバプールの建築学校で教育を受けた。フォスター・アソシエーツで4年間働いたあと、独立して英連邦とフランスで開業した。彼はクリサリス・アーキテクツの創立メンバーの1人であったが、1981年に分かれて、別の関心を追求することにし、ロンドンでイアン・リチー・アソシエーツを設立。会社は軽量構造物、受動型太陽エネルギー、美術とテクノロジーに力を注いでいる。彼の作品は多くの賞を得ており、広く公表され、展覧されている。彼はまた英連邦、フランスおよび日本などで講義をしたこともある。

## JAMES STIRLING + MICHAEL WILFORD + PARTNERS LTD.
### ジェームズ・スターリング + マイケル・ウィルフォード + パートナーズ・リミテッド

address : 8 Fitzroy Square London W1P
         5AH

phone : 01-388-6188

◎ Born in 1926, James Stirling studied at the Liverpool School of Art and the School of Architecture at Liverpool University. He has been in Private practice since 1956, and officially set up with Michael James Wilford in 1971.
◎ Michael Wilford was born in Surbiton, Surrey in 1938 and studied at the Kingston Technical School, the Northern Polytechnic School of Architecture, London, and the Regent Street Polytechnic Planning School in London. Although he has worked with James Stirling since 1960, it was not until 1971 that they set up business together.

◎ 1926年生まれのジェームズ・スターリングはリバプール・スクール・オブ・アートとリバプール大学の建築学部で学んだ。1965年以来個人で開業しており、1971年正式にマイケル・ウィルフォードと組んで開業した。
◎ マイケル・ウィルフォードは1938年、サーレーのサービトンで生まれ、キングストン・テクニカル・スクール、ロンドンのノーザン・ポリテクニック・スクール・オブ・アーキテクチュアおよびロンドンのリージェント・ストリート・ポリテクニック・プランニング・スクールで学んだ。1960年来ジェームズ・スターリングと一緒に仕事をしていながら、ようやく1971年に共同で事業を設立した。

## NICHOLAS GRIMSHAW + PARTNERS LTD.
ニコラス・グリムショウ＋パートナーズ・リミテッド

164…169

address : 118-126 Cavendish Street
London W1M 7EF
phone : 01-631-0869
◎ Nick Grimshaw graduated with honours from the Architectural Association School of Architecture in 1965 and has been in private practice since then. His present firm, Nicholas Grimshaw & Partners Ltd., was established in 1980. Nick Grimshaw built up his riputation in the field of industrial architecture during the 1970's when he received the Financial Times Award for Industrial Architecture and a RIBA award for his work on the Herman Miller building in Bath. Since the establishment of his present firm he widened his scope to include sports and leisure complexes, commercial and retail buildings and projicts inthe field of television and radio.

◎ニック・グリムショウは1965年アーキテクチュラル・アソシエーション・スクール・オブ・アーキテクチュアを優等で卒業し、それ以来ずっと開業している。彼の現在の会社、ニコラス・グリムショウ＋パートナーズ・リミテッドは1980年に設立された。1970年代にファイナンシャル・タイムズ社のインダストリアル・アーキテクチュア賞と、バースのハーマン・ミラー・ビルディングの仕事に対するリバ賞を受けて、工業建築の分野で確固たる名声を築いた。現在の会社を設立してから、彼は活動分野を広げて、スポーツやレジャーの複合施設、商業や小売業の建物、テレビジョンやラジオの分野でのプロジェクトまで含めるようになった。

## POWELL-TUCK, CONNOR + OREFELT LTD.
パウエルータック.コナー＋オルフェルト・リミテッド

175…181

address : 11 Plato Place 72-74 St.
Dionis Road London SW6 4TU
phone : 01-736-9337
◎ This practice was established in 1976. It mainly concentrates on architecture, land-scaping and interior and furniture design. Work they have been involved with range from specially commisioned new-build luxury house and studios is California, shop design in Taiwan, new-build offices and studios in London to recording studios, private housing and the design of chairs and light fittings.

## PAWSON SILVESTRIN
ポーソン・シルヴェストリン

address : 77 New Bond Street London
W1Y 9DB
phone : 01-495-1212
◎ John Pawson was born in Halifax, Yorkshire in 1948 and after joining the family business between 1968 and 1974 continued his studies at the Nagoya University of Commerce, Japan and the Architectural Association in London. He joined forces with Claudio Silvestrin in 1982.
◎ Claudio Silvestrin was born in 1954 and trained in Milan under Professor A.G. Fronzoni, the master of Italian "Architectura Essenziale". He later moved to the University of Philosophy at Bologna and the Architectural Association in London. Before going into partnership with John Pawson in 1982, he was involved with several independant projects and some projects with John Hardy.

## RON ARAD/ONE OFF
ロン・アラッド／ワン・オフ

194…201

address : 39-41 Shelton Street London
WC2
phone : 01-379-7796
◎ Ron Arad was born in Tel Aviv, Israel in 1951 and attended the Jerusalem Academy of Art between 1971 and 1973. Moving to London in 1973, he continued his studies at the Architectural Association from 1974 to 1979. He established One Off Covent Garden, London in 1981, and then started off Ron Arad Associates (Architectural) in 1989.
◎ロン・アラッドは1951年イスラエルのテル・アヴィヴで生まれ、1971年から1973年まで、エルサレム・アカデミー・オブ・アートで学んだ。1973年ロンドンに移り、1974年から1979年までアーキテクチュラル・アソシエーションで勉学を続けた。1981年ロンドンのコヴェント・ガーデンにワン／オフを設立。その後1989年になってロン・アラッド・アソシエーツを始めた。

◎この事務所は1976年に設立された。主として、建築、造園、インテリアと家具のデザインに集中して力を注いでいる。事務所がたずさわった仕事はカリフォルニアにおいて、特別に依嘱された新築の豪邸とスタジオ、台湾における店舗デザイン、ロンドンにおける新築のオフィスとスタジオから、個人の家、椅子や照明器具のデザインにまで広い範囲にわたっている。

170…174

◎ジョン・ポーソンは1948年ヨークシャーのハリファックスで生まれ、1968年から1974年まで家業についたあと、日本の名古屋商科大学とロンドンのアーキテクチュラル・アソシエーションで勉学を続けた。彼は1982年クラウディオ・シルヴェストリンと組むことにした。
◎クラウディオ・シルヴェストリンは1954年に生まれ、ミラノにおいてイタリアの「アーキテットウラ・エッセンツィアーレ」の権威、A・G・フロンゾニ教授のもとで教育を受けた。のちにボローニャの哲学大学とロンドンのアーキテクチュラル・アソシエーションに移った。1982年ジョン・ポーソンと共同事業に入る前、彼は独立したプロジェクト数件とジョン・ハーディと共同でいくつかのプロジェクトにたずさわった。

## RICHARD ROGERS + PARTNERS
リチャード・ロジャース＋パートナーズ

182…193

address : Thames Wharf Studios
Rainville Road London W6
phone : 01-385-1235
◎ Richard Rogers was born in Florence in 1933 and received his training at the Architectural Association in London and then at Yale University. He has had a high-profile in the field of design and architecture since 1963 when he established Team 4 with Norman Foster. The Richard Rogers + Partnership was established in 1977 with John Young, Marco Goldschmied and Mike Davise. Some of their major work includes the redevelopment of Lloyd's of London Headquarters, Inmos Microprocessor factory, PA Technology, the National Gallery extension, Billingsgate Market, Strategic Plan for the Royal Docks in London and the Reuters Data Center. Richard Rogers is a member of the Royal Academy, London and Chairman of the Board of the Tate Gallery.

◎リチャード・ロジャースは1933年フィレンツェで生まれ、ロンドンのアーキテクチュラル・アソシエーション、続いてイエール大学で教育を受けた。ノーマン・フォスターとチム4を設立した。1963年以来、デザインと建築の分野で、明確な立場をとっている。リチャード・ロジャース＋パートナーズは1977年、ジョン・ヤング、マルコ・ゴールドシュミードおよびマイク・ディヴィスが協力して設立した。彼らの主な仕事としてはロイズのロンドン本部再開発、インモス・マイクロプロセッサー工場、PAテクノロジー、国立美術館の拡張、ビリングスゲート・マーケット、ロンドンのロイヤル・ドックのための戦略的プランおよびロイターズ・データ・センターなどがある。リチャード・ロジャースはロンドンの王立美術院会員で、テート美術館委員会の議長でもある。

## STANTON WILLIAMS
スタントン・ウィリアムズ

209...212

address : Studio 9A 17 Heneage Street
London E1 5LJ
phone : 01-247-3171

◎ Alan Stanton graduated with an honours diploma from the Arhitectural Association in London and received an MA in Architecture and Urban design from the University of California, Los Angeles. He is also a member of the Royal Institute of British Architects and a Medallist of the Societe des Architectes Diplome par le Government, Paris. Paul Williams is a BA (Honours) and an MA in 3D Design from the Birmingham College of Art, and a Research Fellow in Museum and Gallery Design at the Yale Arts Centre, USA. Current projects being undertaken by Stanton Williams include the design of a new wing for the National Portrait Gallery, the design of a new museum in Winchester Cathedral and a master plan for development of Hawksmoor's Church and site in St. George-in-the-East, London.

◎ アラン・スタントンはロンドンのアーキテクチュラル・アソシエーションを優等で卒業。ロサンゼルスのカリフォルニア大学から建築と都市デザインの修士号を受けた。またロイヤル・インスティチュート・オブ・ブリティッシュ・アーキテクツの会員であり、パリの政府による建築家資格試験協会のメダリストでもある。ポール・ウィリアムズはバーミンガム・カレッジ・オブ・アートの学士（優等）で３Dデザインの修士である。そしてアメリカのイエール・アート・センターにある博物館および美術館デザインの特別研究員である。スタントンが現在引受けている仕事には、ナショナル・ポートレート・ギャラリーの新しい翼部の設計、ウインチェスター聖堂の新しい博物館の設計およびロンドンのセント・ジョージ・イン・ザ・イーストにおけるホークスムア教会と敷地を開発するためのマスター・プランなどがある。

## TREVOR HORNE ARCHITECTS
トレヴァ・ホーン・アーキテクツ

address : 14a Clerkenwell Green London
EC1R 0DP
phone : 01-250-0893

◎ Trevor Horne is an Englishman who lived abroad. He studied architecture at the University of Toronto and has been responsible for work in large practices in Britain and Canada. He entered private practie in 1983 after taking first prize in the University of Durham Oriental Museum Competition. He is a tutor and visiting critic in various colleges and universities throughout the world, and has had several of his works published in both English and foreign journals.

213...214

◎ トレヴァ・ホーンは海外で暮していたイギリス人である。トロント大学で建築を学び、イギリスとカナダの大きな事務所で責任ある地位にあった。1983年ダラム大学の東洋博物館コンペティションで１等をとったあと開業した。彼は世界の各地でいろいろなカレッジと総合大学で講師や、訪問批評家をしており、仕事のうち数件をイギリス・海外の両方で学会誌に発表している。

## SIMON CONDER ASSOCIATES
サイモン・コンダー・アソシエーツ

202...208

address : 68a Leonard Street London
EC2A 4QX
phone : 01-739-6492

◎ Simon Condor was trained at the Architectural Association School of Architecture and the Royal Collegie of Art Industrial Design Department. He worked in the public sector of Basildon New Town between 1975 and 1982, and then moved onto the London Borough of Lambeth. He established his own practice in 1982. The earlier years of this new practice were dominated by conversion projects which included conversion work on listed houses, but since 1984 the scale of the work-load has expanded to include new-build projects and interior design work ranging between 600sq. ft. and 150,000sq. ft.

◎ サイモン・コンダーはアーキテクチュラル・アソシエーション・スクールとロイヤル・カレッジ・オブ・アートの工業デザイン学部で教育を受けた。1975年から1982年までベイシルドン・ニュー・タウンの公共セクターで働き、その後ロンドンのランベス自治区に移った。新しい仕事の頭初は、リストに記載された住宅の改造作業を含め、改造プロジェクトが主であった。しかし、1984年以来、仕事量の規模が広がって、新築プロジェクトや600平方フィートから150,000平方フィートにおよぶインテリアデザインの仕事も入るようになった。

## TROUGHTON MCASLAN LTD.
トゥローートン・マッカスラン・リミテッド

215...220

address : 186 Campden Hill Road
London W8 7TH
phone : 01-727-2663

◎ Jamie Troughton graduated from Cambridge University in 1975 and subsequently worked for Foster Associates and Richard Rogers & Partners. John McAslan received his training at Edinburgh University and worked in Boston, America, for two years from 1978. He returned to the UK in 1980 and worked for Richard Rogers & Partners until establishing Troughton McAslan Limited with Jamie Troughton in 1983. The workload is split evenly between the two, with Jamie Troughton concentrating on coordinates, financial and planning matters, and John McAslan specializing in design and project management.

◎ ジェミー・トゥロートンは1975年ケンブリッジ大学を卒業し、続いてフォスター・アソシエーツとリチャード・ロジャース＋パートナーズで働いた。ジョン・マッカスランはエジンバラ大学で教育を受け、1978年から２年間アメリカのボストンで働いた。1980年に英連邦に戻り、リチャード・ロジャース＋パートナーズで働いたあと、1983年にジェミー・トゥロートンとトゥロートン・マッカスラン・リミテッドを設立。仕事量は２人の間で平等に分けられ、ジェミー・トゥロートンはコーディネート、財務や計画の問題に力を集中し、ジョン・マッカスランはデザインとプロジェクト管理を専門にしている。

## WICKHAM+ASSOCIATES ARCHITECTS
ウィッカム+アソシエーツ・アーキテクツ

address : 4 Crawford Passage London
　　　　　EC1R 3DP
phone : 01-833-2631
◎ The Wickham & Associates practice was established in 1971 by Tess Wickham, Jamie Cambell, Brendan Woods and Mard Willmott. Since the firm was created they have accepted commisions that range from the interior design of bars, restaurants and clubs as well as many residential interiors, a clinic and planning studies for the Covent Garden Market and Banstead Hospital. They are currently involved in a wide range of work that includes planning studies, interior fitting, a new city block by Tower Bridge, a block of flats, two office buildings and two factories.

◎ウィッカム＋アソシエーツ・アーキテクツは1971年、テス・ウィッカム、ジェミー・キャンベル、ブレンダン・ウッズおよびマーク・ウィルモットにより設立された。会社が創立されてから、彼らは数多くの住民のインテリアばかりでなく、バーやレストランやクラブのインテリア・デザインからクリニックやコベント・ガーデン・マーケットとバンステッド病院のプラン研究まで多岐にわたる依嘱を受けてきた。現在彼らはプラン研究、インテリアの設備、タワー・ブリッジ近辺の新しい都市ブロック、フラット式共同住宅のブロック、オフィス・ビル2棟および工場2件などの広い範囲の仕事に専念している。

## WILLIAM ALSOP+ JOHN LYALL ARCHITECTS
ウィリアム・アルソップ＋ジョン・ライアル・アーキテクツ

address : The Power House, Alpha Place
　　　　　London SW3 5SZ
phone : 01-351-3166
◎ William Alsop was born in Northampton in 1947, and John Lyall in Essex in 1949. They established the practice together in January 1981 and have built up a reputation for interesting architecture at low costs. They are well known in German and France as a result of this reputation, and the practice is steadily expanding. The number of architects working for the practice fluctuates from time-to-time, but it averages out at about ten people.

◎ウィリアム・アルソップは1947年ノーザンプトンの生まれ、ジョン・ライアルは1949年エセックスの生まれである。2人は1981年共同で開業し、おもしろい建築を低コストで建てることで評判になった。この評判のお陰で、2人は西ドイツとフランスでよく知られており、事業は着々と拡大している。事務所で働く建築家の数には時折変動があるが、平均すると約10人である。

## ZAHA HADID
ザハ・ハディド

address : Studio 9 10 Bowling Green
　　　　　Lane London EC1
phone : 01-253-5147
◎ Zaha Hadid attended the Achitectural Association and then worked with the Office of Metropolitan Architecture before setting up her own practice. She worded on several projects at the same time as teaching full-time at the Architectural Association, and presently works out of a converted Victorian schoolhouse in Clerkenwell, London. She is currently working on an office building and housing block for IBM in Berlin, and a vertical retail building and studio office in Tokyo; the latter of which is soon to commence construction.

◎ザハ・ハディドはアーキテクチュラル・アソシエーションで学び、その後オフィス・オブ・メトロポリタン・アーキテクチュアで開業するまで働いた。アーキテクチュラル・アソシエーションでフルタイムの教師をするかたわら、いくつかのプロジェクトに従事していた。現在はロンドンのクラーケンウェルにある、ヴィクトリア時代の校舎を改造した建物を仕事場として、目下ベルリンで、IBMのためのオフィス・ビルディングと住宅ブロック、および東京で縦長の小売店ビルディング兼スタジオ・オフィスに従事している。東京でもまもなく建設にはいる予定のものがある。

# AFTERWORD

◎In recent years, the economical development of Japan has led to the situation where a great amount of surplus money is moved to real estate investment. This phenomenon is creating an alltime boom in architecture, all of which is based within the principles of a strong economy. Society has forgotten that design is there to serve the populace with a better quality of life. Altough the effect is not quite as tragic as in Japan, as business develops situations similar to the Docklands are born. It can be said that the style of buildings that are being created there are in accordance to the principles of the economy. In direct constrast, the architects introduced within these covers champion the cause of quality buildings. They urge their own beliefs onto the buildings. Amongst these architects are James Stirling, who took part in CIAM 1950 and has continually produced high quality architecture such as the engineering building faculty for the Leicester University, and Peter Cook and Ron Herron who have successively produced imaginative architecture as members of Archigrams. For example, Peter Cook presented the Plug-In City in 1964 and Ron Herron the Walking City in the same year.

◎Their technology based on a Utopian-style movement was handed over to successive architects such as Foster and Rogers. Commanding the 20th century technology, they repeated their experiments and adventures to open up the way to high quality modernization. With the above-mentioned pioneers as teachers, the times are now producing a new movement of architects such as Peter Wilson, William Alsop, Nigel Coats, Armstrong and Chipperfield. With this drastic change in the generation the next age of architecture is upon us. Behind these progressive styles is the architectural education and discussions that support the architecture demands. Especially, the A.A. School (The Architectural Association School of Architecture) is the place where architects and critics from all over the world gather to air and exchange their thoughts and opinions, the discussions on postmodernization and construction was repeated there.

◎The flow of modernization in England was followed in order to compile this volume. Aa a general rule I visited each piece of architecture selected for inclusion in the book and requested the cooperation of all involved. I also received the advice of both Peter Cook, my professor at A.A. School, and John Welsh of the Designer's Journal.

◎I would like to offer my special thanks to Tim Toomey who was kept busy organizing the material collection, etc. This volume is the third edition in a series which includes "Italian Design" and "Italian Interior Design". Last but not least I would like to send my sincerest gratitude to Toru Kaiho, the designer, for his sharp arrangements, and also to Kakuzo Akahira of Graphic-sha Publishing who was kind enough to give me advise when needed.

November 1989

Fumio Shimizu

250

# あとがきにかえて

近年日本での金余り現象は、土地、建物への投資を活発化させ、都市においては空前の建築ブームとなって現れている。その大半は経済原理優先の建築が進められるため、「高いクオリティーのための生活やよりよいライフスタイルのために」といった、社会が人に対してどのようにデザインすべきかが忘れられている。

ドッグランズにおいても、日本ほどではないが、同じような状況がみられる。そこにかかわる建築家たちも経済原理によっているといえる。

ここに登場する建築家たちは、建築のクオリティーを高めようと、みずからの信念に従ってデザインをしている。それらの建築家たちには、1950年代の CIAM に参加し、1959年のレスター大学工学部棟の提案などクオリティーの高い建築を発表しつづけているジェームズ・スターリング、アーキグラムのメンバーとしてイマジナリー・アーキテクチュアを発表しつづけたピーター・クック、また、ロン・ヘロンがいる。

ピーター・クックは、1964年 plug-in city を発表し、ロン・ヘロンも、同年 Walking City を発表している。彼らのテクノロジーを基にした、ユートピアン的運動は、フォスター、ロジャースなどの建築へとつながっている。彼らは、20世紀のテクノロジーを駆使して、実験と冒険を繰りかえし、質の高いモダニズムの途を切り開いている。

また、これらの先駆者たちを師として、ピーター・ウィルソン、ウィリアム・アルソップ、ナイジェル・コーツ、アームストロング、チッパーフィールドなど、新しい建築家たちが新しい動きをみせている。このようなドラマチックな世代交代とともに、次期の建築がつくりだされている。その裏には建築にたいする、情熱（インスージアズム）や建築への思索、感受性をサポートする建築教育や議論の場がある。特に、A.A.スクール（アーキテクチュラル・アソシエイション・スクール・オブ・アーキテクチュア）は、世界の建築家や批評家が集まり、情熱的に議論・批評が繰りかえされる場所でもある。そこでは十数年前から「ポストモダン」や「デコンストラクション」についての議論が繰りかえされていた。

本書では、建築の世界の中心をロンドンと位置づけさせるほどに注目させた、発明的で実験的な建築家たちと現在活躍している若い世代の建築家たちに焦点をあて、イギリスのモダニズムの流れを追いながら編集した。作品の選定にあたっては、原則として、建築家を個別に尋ねて協力を仰いだ。また、私の A.A.スクール当時の教授であったピーター・クック氏、デザイナーズ・ジャーナルのジョン・ウェルシュ氏に助言を仰いだ。マテリアルの収集など、オーガナイズに奔走していただいた、ティム・トゥーミー氏には、特にお世話になった。

最後に、シャープな装慎をしていただいたブック・デザイナーの海保透氏、また『イタリアン・デザイン』、『イタリアン・インテリア』につづいて、企画・進行・助言と大変お世話になったグラフィック社の赤平覚三氏に心から御礼申し上げます。

1989年11月

清水文夫

**Fumio Shimizu**

Born in Shimane in 1950.
Educated at the Shibaura Institute of Technology in Tokyo, Architectural Association School of Architecture in London, and at the Politechnico Di Milano.
Worked with Takefumi Aida from 1981 to 1984
and Matteo Thun from 1984 to 1986.
Founded Shimizu Fumio Architects in 1988, involving the fields of Architecture, ID and interior design in Tokyo and Milano.
Has written discourses for several magazines and books, such as "The Itarian Design — Descendants of Leonardo da Vinci —", "The Italian Interior", "Architectural Drawing: The Art and The Process", etc.

**清水文夫**

1950年、島根県生まれ。
芝浦工業大学、A.A.スクール、ミラノ工科大学にて建築を学ぶ。
1981年より相田武文設計研究所、
1984年よりステューディオ・マッテオ・トゥン、
1988年、清水文夫アーキテクツを設立、現在に至る。
東京とミラノで、
建築、ID、インテリア・デザインの各分野で
精力的な活動を行いつつ各誌で健筆をふるっている。
編著書に、
《イタリアン・デザイン—レオナルド・ダ・ヴィンチの末裔たち》、
《イタリアン・インテリア》、
《現代建築家ドローイング集成アメリカ編》他

**Deyan Sudjic**

Born in London in 1952 of Yugoslav parents. Educated at the University of Edinburgh, taking his diploma in architecture in 1976.
He has worked as a critic and journalist ever since. For eight years he was architecture critic for the London Sunday Times, as well as contributing to a range of specialist architecture and desigh publications. In 1983 he helped to found Blueprint, a monthly magazine of architecture and design, of which he is currently editor.
In 1987 he was joint curator of the Royal Academy's exhibition on the work of Richard Rogers, James Stirling and Norman Foster. And in 1988 he was curator of Metropolis, an exhibition at the Institute of Contemporary Arts in London, bringing together the work of Zaha Hadid, Nigel Coates, Ron Arad, Future Systems, Weil and Taylor and John Pawson.
He has published a number of books, including Cult Objects, and New Directions in British Architecture. He is currently writing a book on urbanism in the twentieth century.

**ダヤン・スジック**

1952年、ロンドン生まれ。
1976年、エジンバラ大学にて建築を学ぶ。
評論家、ジャーナリストとして現在も活躍中。
8年にわたり、ロンドン・サンデー・タイムに建築評論家として、
建築やデザイン書籍のコラムを担当。
1983年、建築とデザインの月刊誌ブループリントの創刊にさいし、
編集長として参与。
1987年、ロイヤル・アカデミーの共同館長としてリチャード・ロジャース、ジェームズ・スターリング、ノーマン・フォスターの
作品展を開催。
1988年、メトロポリス美術館の館長として、コンテンポラリー・アーツ協会展をロンドンで開催、
ザハ・ハディド、ナイジェル・コーツ、ロン・アラッド、
フューチャー・システムズ、ワイル＋テーラー、ジョン・ポーソンの作品を紹介した。
著書に
《カルト・オブジェクト》《ブリティッシュ・アーキテクチュアの新しい傾向》
他
現在、20世紀の都市生活についての本を執筆中である。

**Fumio Shimizu**

# THE BRITISH ARCHITECTURE & INTERIOR
## ブリティッシュ・アーキテクチュア&インテリア

1989年12月25日初版第1刷発行

定価13,000円(本体12,621円)

編著者　清水文夫©＋ダヤン・スジック©

発行者　久世利郎

印刷所　凸版印刷株式会社

製本所　和田製本株式会社

写植　株式会社三山綜合システム　株式会社プロスタディオ

発行所　株式会社グラフィック社
〒102　東京都千代田区九段北1-9-12
電話＝03-263-4318　振替・東京3-114345

落丁・乱丁はお取替え致します。
ISBN4-7661-0545-1 C3052 P13000E